Light from the East

ICONS IN LITURGY AND PRAYER

Light
from the East

ICONS IN LITURGY AND PRAYER

❧

by
Michael Evdokimov

Translation and Introduction by
Robert Smith, F.S.C.

Paulist Press
New York/Mahwah, N.J.

Artwork on pages 5, 30, 40, 65, and 89 are courtesy: Scala/Art Resource, NY. Artwork on page 37 is courtesy Erich Lessing/Art Resource, NY. Artwork on page 47 is courtesy: Beniaminson/Art Resource, NY. Other artwork is courtesy of Brothers of the Christian Schools/De La Salle Institute.

Unless otherwise noted, the scripture quotations outlined herein are from the New Revised Standard Version Bible, copyright © 1989 by the Division of Christian Education of the National Council of Churches of Christ in the U.S.A. Used by permission.

Prayers are taken from a variety of sources: *Troparia and Kondakia* copyright © 1984 by Monks of New Skete; Liturgical Music, Series 1: Great Feasts, Volume 2, *Dormition of the Theotokos* copyright © 1986 by Monks of New Skete; Liturgical Music, Series 1: Great Feasts, Volume 3, *Birth of the Theotokos* copyright © 1986 by Monks of New Skete; *Passion and Resurrection,* copyright © 1995 by Monks of New Skete; and *Sighs of the Spirit* copyright © 1997 by Monks of New Skete. Used by permission.

Cover design by Cynthia Dunne
Book design by Saija Autrand, Faces Type & Design

Library of Congress Cataloging-in-Publication Data

Evdokimov, Michael.
    Light from the East: icons in liturgy and prayer / by Michael Evdokimov; with translator's introduction by Robert Smith.
        p. cm.
    ISBN 0-8091-4278-3 (alk. paper)
    1. Church year.   2. Orthodox Eastern Church—Liturgy.   3. Icons—Meditations.   4. Orthodox Eastern Church—Prayer-books and devotions—English.   5. Spiritual life—Orthodox Eastern Church.   I. Title.
    BX376.3 .E93 2003
    246'.53—dc21

                                                                    2003011213

Part of this book was published as
Lumières d'Orient
by Droguet & Ardant
Groupe Fleurus Mame
15/27, Rue Moussorgski
75895, Paris, France

Published by Paulist Press
997 Macarthur Boulevard
Mahwah, New Jersey 07430

www.paulistpress.com

Printed and bound in the
United States of America

Table of Contents

Acknowledgments...viii

Introduction ix

Part One: The Yearly Cycle of Feasts

The Birth of the Mother of God SEPTEMBER 8.........................2
 The Icon of the Birth of the Mother of God
 Prayers

The Exaltation of the Cross SEPTEMBER 14 7
 The Icon of the Exaltation of the Cross
 Prayers

The Presentation of the Virgin in the Temple NOVEMBER 21 14
 The Icon of the Presentation of the Virgin in the Temple
 Prayers

Christmas DECEMBER 25 18
 The Icon of the Nativity of the Lord
 Prayers

Epiphany JANUARY 6..23
 The Icon of the Epiphany of the Lord
 Prayers

The Holy Meeting of the Lord FEBRUARY 2 28
    The Icon of the Holy Meeting of the Lord
    Prayers

The Annunciation MARCH 25 33
    The Icon of the Annunciation
    Prayers

The Entry into Jerusalem SIXTH SUNDAY OF LENT 38
    The Icon of the Entry into Jerusalem
    Prayers

The Resurrection EASTER SUNDAY 43
    The Icon of Easter
    Prayers

The Ascension ASCENSION THURSDAY 48
    The Icon of the Ascension
    Prayers

Pentecost SECOND SUNDAY AFTER THE ASCENSION 52
    The Icon of Pentecost
    Prayers

The Transfiguration AUGUST 6 58
    The Icon of the Transfiguration
    Prayers

The Dormition AUGUST 15 62
    The Icon of the Dormition
    Prayers

Part Two: Icons in Prayer

Notes on the Icon of the Trinity 69
    Rublev's Icon of the Trinity
    Prayers

On Prayer 74

Worship in the Orthodox Church 80

Notes on the Icon of Christ 82
    The Icon of Christ
    Prayers

Notes on the Icon of the Mother of God: "Mother Most Tender" 86
    The Icon of the Mother of God
    Prayers

Afterword 90
    A Book for Those in Search of God   91
    Preliminary Remarks on the Liturgy: Heaven on Earth   92
    Liturgy and the Bible   93
    Can Modern Men and Women Relate to the Liturgy?   93
    Thoughts on the Power of Beauty: The Lord Is Clothed in Splendor   94
    Icons: Places Where God's Beauty Dwells   95

Acknowledgments

It is probably not possible to mention everyone who has been directly or indirectly helpful in bringing this translation to the light of day. One name is certainly primary: Dennis McManus. Were it not for his persistence and vigor in breaking down doors that seemed permanently closed, nothing would have happened. Other names deserving mention are: Ann Martin, Richard Schmechel, Steven Werlin, Kevin Topper, Dimitri Fotos, and Chester Burke. In other important ways my superiors in the California Province of the De La Salle Christian Brothers and Arturo Brillemburg have been generous.

Introduction

❧

This book, *Light from the East: Icons in Liturgy and Prayer,* was written by a Russian Orthodox priest, Father Michael Evdokimov. In it he seeks to draw prayerful attention to the spiritual riches of the Byzantine liturgy. The book shows how the prayers and the icons used to worship God, especially on the twelve great feasts of the liturgical year, nourish spiritual life and lead believers even in this life to share in the divine life.

Though the author sets before his readers beliefs and practices common to Orthodox people everywhere in the world, he does so in a distinctly personal way. He speaks of the spiritual meaning of each feast of the Byzantine liturgical year, and he frames his personal remarks with prayers from the liturgy itself. He also adds quotations from distinctively Russian sources as would be expected from one brought up on that rich Orthodox tradition.

Part one of the book presents an icon for each of the twelve great feasts of the year. Part two presents the icon of the Trinity, the center of all Christian worship, the icon of Christ, and the icon of the Virgin, "Mother Most Tender."

Preceding each icon there is a brief setting forth of what the reader can hope to find in the icon. Here the guidance Father Michael gives us is of the highest value. Much that a casual reader might miss is supplied. When we follow along with the explanation, we are gently being given wonderful spiritual guidance.

Facing the page on which the icon appears there are prayers that can be said while meditating on the icon. On the following page or pages there are in some instances quotations from spiritual writers from all ages of Christianity concerning the feast the Church invites us to celebrate.

The Byzantine liturgy has its roots in the worship of the Church in Jerusalem from the earliest times. Its central nucleus was the gathering each Saturday night in prayerful expectation of Christ's return. The prayers were mainly the psalms and canticles of the Old Testament, culminating in a reading of the gospel of the Resurrection. When midnight came and Christ had not yet returned, the Eucharist was celebrated in obedience to his command to do so in commemoration of him.

Around this central nucleus over the past sixteen hundred years has grown an incomparable collection of hymns and prayers celebrating God's intervention in the life of the world, his saving work of bringing fallen humanity into a sharing of his own triune life. What is most to be remarked about the Byzantine liturgical tradition is that it never loses sight of this essential truth. Nothing trivial or secondary is allowed to obscure the fact that the prime purpose of the Church on earth is to join with the heavenly community in the worship of a God who wants us to share his own divine life.

As we see in this book, there are twelve great feasts celebrated during the year. Each of them commemorates some aspect of God's merciful involvement in our life. Each feast celebrates some historical event—Christ's Resurrection, his Nativity, his Transfiguration, for example—but the emphasis is not on something external to us that happened to Christ or the apostles long ago. Each event represents a reaching down by God to us in order to bring us back to him. Nothing is ever allowed to obscure this central exchange. Christ rose to raise up all the race of Adam. When he was born, he showed that he had taken on human nature so that we might be transformed into sharers of the divine nature.

There is a celebration for the birth of God's mother, but in the central collect for that feast the Church speaks of her birth as the introductory act of God's plan to save all humanity.

There are several celebrations (not part of the twelve great feasts) of the life and death of Saint John the Baptist, but the emphasis is on his pointing to Christ, whose work was to take away the sins of the world. Innumerable other saints are also commemorated, especially the prophets, martyrs, and ascetic saints who lived in the desert, but they have a more moderate place in the liturgy compared to the great events in the history of our salvation. The stories of these saints are seen as examples of how the Holy Spirit works in the lives of men and women to raise them to God. One expression used to describe the ascetic saints is that they are the "lyre of the Holy Spirit," because the Spirit played within their minds and hearts to make them godlike.

It is the liturgy understood in this way that is the subject of Father Michael's book.

The word "icon" too can be misinterpreted. Catholics especially may think that it means something like the statues or other "holy pictures" found in their churches and homes, or even that icons have kinship with what are unquestionably great works of art, the religious paintings of the Renaissance. This is not so.

An icon is essentially the work of a painter who, after fasting and prayer, succeeds in conveying visually some aspect of God's involvement in our life. Traditionally, an icon painter was set aside for his work in a ceremony derived from the Office of the Transfiguration, the mystery of God's glory becoming manifest. The painter depends on inspiration, but what he needs derives from the Holy Spirit sent into our hearts to open them to the meaning of God's word. Any impulse not directed in this way to the service of what God has said to us in scripture and tradition is foreign to icons.

When one looks at an icon, one has the sense that God is looking back. Our whole person is involved. What the prayers and music of a feast convey through the ears, the icon conveys visually.

Father Michael's purpose in writing this book was to give French-speaking Orthodox faithful the opportunity to meditate on the texts and icons used in the annual cycle of the liturgy and thereby deepen their participation in the prayer of the Church. The present translation may do the same for those whose language is English.

The initial motive prompting this translation was the hope that *Light from the East: Icons in Liturgy and Prayer* might also serve a wider purpose. Western Christians, especially Catholics, Episcopalians, and others who have a formal liturgical tradition akin in its recurrent structure to that of the East might, by reading through this book, be helped to a deeper understanding of their own tradition and so led to a more profound spiritual life. It would seem that Catholics especially, since all the feasts talked about here are also celebrated in the Catholic calendar, might compare their understanding of those feasts with what the Byzantine texts put forward as ways to God. The possibility of this enrichment ought to be an incentive for a prayerful reading of this book in the presence of each of the icons.

As a matter of fact, the immediate impetus for doing this translation was a startling sentence in a recent letter, *Orientale Lumen* (*OL*; Vatican Press, May 2, 1995), written to Catholics by the present pope: "The first need of Catholics is to be familiar with the ancient tradition [of the Eastern Church] so as to be nourished by it."

The first need of Catholics? What makes him say something so extreme? How can he feel justified in doing so?

The pope's reasons are bound up with the mission that is central to his life, his desire to bring the world answers to the questions that most concern it. "The cry of [those] seeking meaning for their lives . . . The women and men of today are asking us to show them Christ . . . Letting the world ask us its questions, listening with humility and tenderness, in full solidarity with those who express them, we are called upon to show in word and deed today the immense riches that our Churches preserve in the coffers of our traditions" (*OL*, p. 7).

It is because of his sense of pastoral mission that this most missionary-minded of all modern popes turns his mind to the East. "In contemplating [the tradition of the Eastern Church], before my eyes appear elements of great significance for a fuller and more thorough understanding of the Christian experience. Those elements are capable of giving a more complete Christian response to the expectations of men and women of today" (*OL*, p. 9).

The pope has by no means forgotten the riches of the Western tradition nor is he unaware that the Western Church has produced saints in every century of its existence. He himself has canonized more of them than all the other popes together. Despite these facts, he feels it necessary to say: "In the study of revealed truth, East and West have used different methods and approaches in understanding and confessing divine things. It is hardly surprising, then, if sometimes one tradition comes nearer to a full appreciation of some aspects of the mystery of revelation than the other, or has expressed them better. In such cases, these various theological formulations are often to be considered complementary rather than conflicting" (*OL*, p. 9).

What are these truths the East has expressed better and that the world is waiting to hear? The pope defers to the bishops of the Eastern Church and says it is for them rather than for him to expound those truths, but he quotes Vatican II to give in brief form what he thinks these distinctive truths are:

> Everyone knows with what love the Eastern Christians celebrate the sacred liturgy and especially the eucharistic mystery, source of the Church's life and pledge of future glory. In this mystery the faithful, united with their bishops, have access to God the Father through the Son, the Word made flesh who suffered and was glorified in the outpouring of the Holy Spirit. And so, made "sharers of the divine nature," they enter into communion with the most Holy Trinity. (Second Vatican Ecumenical Council Decree on Ecumenism, *Unitatis Redintegratio*, chap. 3, no. 15)

The pope goes on to restate this ideal, an aspect of the Eastern tradition that is all-important in his eyes:

> These features describe the Eastern outlook of the Christian. His or her goal is participation in the divine nature through communion with the most Holy Trinity. In this view . . . is outlined . . . the concept of salvation according to the divine plan as it is presented by Eastern theology . . . Participation in trinitarian life takes place through the liturgy, and in a special way through the Eucharist . . . Eastern theology attributes a very special role to the Holy Spirit: through the power of the Spirit who dwells in man, deification already begins on earth; the creature is transfigured and God's kingdom inaugurated. (*OL*, 11f.)

So it is not concerning some secondary matter that the pope thinks Western Christians need to look to the East for nourishment. We need to be inspired by the Eastern vision of salvation itself as a share in the life of the Trinity that we must come to share with the members of the Oriental Church.

We can come to know about these essential truths by meditating on the words of the Byzantine liturgy. It is principally through that liturgy that those truths have been transmitted and preserved. We can, under the guidance of the Holy Spirit, make the sentiments of the Byzantine liturgical prayers our own and thus enter more deeply into the trinitarian life by the Eucharist.

The West has its own rich traditions and its own discoveries about how to lead a life pleasing to God. During the nearly thousand years we have been separated from the East, we have achieved certain valuable insights about the responsibility of human society for all its members. This is a way of saying that we have made advances in learning how to love our neighbor as ourselves. This is not, however, the place to speak of the good things of the West. The pope is directing us to look at the very heart of religion, intimacy with God.

These words need to be expounded much more fully. Father Michael's book does so in an admirable fashion. Let the reader go slowly through the feasts of the year with their icons and the texts found in this book. A Catholic or a Protestant reader need not trust in advance the pope's words about our first need. Each one can test for himself or herself whether the evidence provided in this book is sufficient to justify the opinion of John Paul II.

It may be useful to expand on some of the things that have been said about the way this book is arranged.

On the page facing each icon there are prayers that one can say in the presence of the icon. These prayers are all from the liturgy of the feast and are given in the translation of the Monks of New Skete who have graciously given their permission for this use. The prayers do not appear in this form in the French edition, but it was thought useful to have both prayers and icon close enough together that they can combine to help the reader.

In some instances there then follow quotations from witnesses of tradition that Father Michael has chosen to give us a deeper sense of the feast.

At the end of the book there is an "Afterword" by Father Michael on prayer and the spiritual life. The reader will find a most instructive and meaningful series of thoughts on these matters. This book would be valuable if it contained nothing but this final section.

The order just described is not that of the French edition. What is presented here as Father Michael's "Afterword" appears as an introduction in the original version. This is understandable, because the French edition was expressly addressed to those who had been familiar with the Byzantine liturgy all their lives. Father Michael could draw on their experience to make what he said on prayer meaningful.

Since this English translation hopes to reach Catholics and others who may not be familiar with the Byzantine liturgy, it seemed better to start with the feasts of the year and then talk about the kind of religious experience this liturgy helps bring about.

The reader may wonder if this kind of departure from the original form of the book might not be disrespectful to the work of Fr. Michael. He was not disturbed by the idea of change. When asked if modifications might be permitted, he replied, almost before the questioner finished speaking, "The translation must be adapted for the use of those for whom it is intended." He said this with all the same warmth and kindness the reader will find when he reads Father Michael's words on prayer and the liturgy.

The Liturgical Year

Light from the East: Icons in Liturgy and Prayer speaks of the high moments of the Byzantine liturgy, the twelve great feasts of the year. Stress is laid on the journey through Lent to Easter, the Ascension and the feast of Pentecost when the revelation of the Trinity reaches its highest point. A growing realization of how these prayers and icons help us share in the life of the Holy Trinity will be the reward a reader can expect from a slow, prayerful reading of Father Michael's book. One obvious way of doing this is to space our readings throughout the liturgical year. The Western Church celebrates all the feasts discussed in this book, but their meaning and relative importance in the East and the West are often different. Meditating on these differences will, as was said above, be instructive. One need not give up the acquisitions of the West; rather, in addition, one can avail oneself of the light that comes from the East. What we learn from the East will complement what we already know.

Some of the feasts talked about are of great importance in both the East and the West. That is clearly the case for Easter and Christmas and increasingly so for Pentecost (which the Russians refer to as "The Trinity").

Since the Easter Vigil was restored in the West a generation ago, Catholics see Easter much more like the Orthodox do. It is of course a triumphant event in Christ's life, but it is inseparably linked with immortality and salvation for each of us individually. The two liturgies of this feast, the Eastern and the Western, are now, since Vatican II, close in ways that emphasize this linkage.

The trinitarian dimension of the Baptism of Christ, his Transfiguration, the Ascension, and Pentecost is more salient in the consciousness of Orthodox faithful than it seems to be in the West. The same can be said of the feast of the Dormition of the Virgin (the Assumption, in language familiar to Catholics).

Priests will find help for their homilies if they look at the emphasis the East places on each feast and then compare that with the insights of the Roman tradition. All of us will find rich inspiration for our prayers and meditation. Parents will derive assistance in guiding their children to enter with their hearts and imaginations into the mysteries these feasts celebrate. What is begun in infancy can develop year after year. A mind formed this way will have something that can be a support for all of life, including its end.

Those who participate in the growing movement of Perpetual Adoration can, if they are inspired to do so, be ideal readers of this book. Following it meditatively over three years cannot fail to have a profound effect. To prepare oneself to meditate, it will be useful to begin by reading slowly and devoutly the prayer that accompanies the icon of the Trinity. That prayer precedes every public prayer of the Eastern Church. A bishop, in recommending it as a beginning for private prayer, described its use as a purification, even a necessary purification of our heart, before we address God himself.

Neither this book nor the quotations from the present pope used to show its relevance are directly concerned with the reunion of the churches. This small book is being presented to help English-speaking Christians, both Eastern and Western, to appreciate more fully the riches of the Byzantine liturgy. Reading Father Michael's book may, however, indirectly contribute to removing one obstacle to unity. It should, for instance, help to combat the smugness and lack of interest that Catholics sometimes show toward a goal for which Our Lord prayed. Who would not want to be one with people who pray in the ways Father Michael tells us of?

Robert Smith, F.S.C.

PART ONE

The Yearly Cycle of Feasts

The Birth of the Mother of God

SEPTEMBER 8

❧ Your birth, O Theotokos, has filled the world with joy, for there rose from you the sun of justice, Christ, our God. He destroyed the curse and replaced it with a blessing, thus confounding death by giving us eternal life.

—Troparion of the Feast

The great work of redemption begins with Mary. "Mary comes into the world, and with her the world is renewed. She is born and the Church is covered with beauty" (Vespers). The most often repeated text of the feast links her with the birth of Jesus: "Your birth, Mother of God, reveals joy to all the universe, for it is from you that the Sun of Justice, Christ our Savior, rose." Other texts celebrate Mary as the temple where God dwells: "You contained in your womb one of the Persons of the Holy Trinity, Christ the King, Whom every creature sings."

The Byzantine liturgical year starts September first. The last great feast of this year is the Assumption (Dormition) on August fif-teenth, and the first important feast of the new year is the Birth of the Mother of God. The way the calendar year is arranged points to Mary's importance for the whole economy of our salvation. How fitting it is that her birth is the first great feast each year. The verses sung at this feast are full of references to a joy that fills the hearts of all the ancestors of Christ on the fulfillment of their hopes. Hymns sung at Vespers mention the root of Jesse and describe Adam as leaping with gladness. Eve exults, while David plays on his harp, shouts for joy, and blesses God. Christ is properly called "the son of David" and "the new Adam," because in Christ fallen humanity has been regenerated.

All this theological richness shines out from the icon of this feast. Ann, who was previously sterile, is stretched out in a manner suitable for someone who has just given birth. Midwives are in attendance, and one of them is washing the child in water. Joachim has come to greet his wife. The red in his cloak corresponds to the color of hers. The hands of the temple priests are outstretched in blessing over the child who, though not in the center of the

icon, occupies a place made prominent by the whiteness of her swaddling clothes. The attention both parents are paying to their daughter is a response to the fulfillment God has given to their conjugal love. Over husband and wife is built the temple where one can draw near to the mystery of God with deepest joy. They say: "Adam and Eve, share the joy that has come to us on this day, for if you by that ancient treason have closed the gates of Paradise, a fruit has been given to us, Mary, whose divine child opens them up for all."

Prayers ∽ SEPTEMBER 8

What is the festive song we hear Joachim and Anna celebrate in the liturgy for today?

Today God who rests on spiritual thrones prepares himself a throne on earth, for he whose wisdom once made the heavens firm, in his love for mankind prepares himself a living heaven. From a barren root he makes a living branch come forth: none other than his mother! O God of wonders, glory to you.

Today is the day of the Lord! Rejoice, you people everywhere! For the bridal chamber of light, the book of the word of life, comes from the womb, and the East Gate, newly born, awaits the entrance of the great priest. For she alone brings into the world the one and only Christ, for the salvation of our souls.

Today barren Anna brings forth the child of God, foreordained from all generations as the dwelling and maker of all, Christ our God, thus fulfilling the divine plan, for through her have we been formed anew, brought from corruption to life without end.

Today has the holy Virgin come, being born of her mother's barrenness, overshadowed mountain from which salvation comes forth. Come, let us sing her praises, for she bore the Savior of the world.

The Nativity of the Virgin. Seventeenth-century icon. Rubliev Museum, Moscow, Russia. Courtesy of Scala/Art Resource, NY.

Let us who hold virginity in high esteem, who strive for purity of heart and mind and body, let us lovingly welcome the boast of virgins everywhere. She is the fountain of life that gushes forth from the flinty rock, the bush that bursts into bloom from barren earth, the bush that burns with immortal fire, that purifies and fills our soul with light.

❧

༄ The joy of all the world shines forth for us, the far-famed Virgin, born of Joachim and Anna. Because of her great goodness she has become the living temple of God, in truth acknowledged as the only Theotokos. By her prayers, O Christ, grant peace to this world of yours, and to our souls, great mercy.

—Liturgy of the Day

༄ Mary is the daughter of Joachim and Anna, the "righteous and holy ancestors of God" [terms used to describe them in the Byzantine liturgy] who were ashamed that they had no children. Jewish people regarded childlessness as a disgrace. One day when they were praying with sadness about their sterility, an angel appeared and announced they were to have a daughter chosen by God for a magnificent role in his plans for the world. The child would come to gladden their old age in the same way that another couple faithful in following the ways of the Lord, Abraham and Sara, had been given a son destined to carry out God's designs. The removal of sterility has, of course, a symbolic meaning and it applies directly to us. "Come, you who believe, let us glorify him who has just been born of a mother who was sterile in order to remove the sterility of our nature."

—Vespers of the Day

The Exaltation of the Cross

SEPTEMBER 14

A strict fast is prescribed for the day of the Exaltation of the Cross. This is the rule for all feasts commemorating the Passion of Our Lord. Though this penitential aspect belongs to the feast, it is also true that a sense of forgiveness, of resurrection, and of joy always accompanies these feelings of penance, of death, and of sadness. In the hymns of Matins we continually hear both these thoughts: "Through the Cross joy comes into the world." Our Savior has told us that if we love him and want to follow him we must take up our cross. How else can there be a bridge between the tiny, malformed persons we would recognize ourselves to be if we saw ourselves clearly and the beautiful and as yet not realized persons we want to become? It is not our own cross that will save us, but the Passion of Jesus who died on a cross that encompasses all the crosses and all the sufferings of all people. This feast should be an occasion to think of what role Our Lord's death on a cross plays in our own life.

The powerful words of the texts sung on this feast bring to our attention a profusion of thoughts. First there is a reference to light:

"Enlighten us by your splendor, O life-giving Cross" (Vespers). Then there is a constantly recurring comparison between the wood of the first tree which brought death and the wood of the Cross, giver of life: "Because he tasted of the fruit of the tree, the first man brought corruption on himself, but we who dwell on earth have discovered the wood of the Cross for our salvation" (Matins). This saving role of wood now extends to all the trees on earth (somewhat in the way the water of the Jordan at Christ's Baptism extends to all liquids in the world): "Let all the trees of the forest whose nature has been made holy now rejoice, because Christ who made that nature has been stretched out on a Cross" (Matins).

This feast was established to commemorate a twofold event whose historical reality cannot be confirmed, but which remains useful because of the symbolic power that legendary events acquire by their incorporation into the liturgy. The first event was the appearance of the Cross to Constantine at the time of his victory over Maxentius. In the following year, A.D. 313, Constantine established freedom of religion throughout the Roman Empire. This was a defeat for idol worship and allowed the Church to emerge from the era of the catacombs.

The second event was the discovery of the Cross by the Empress Helena and her presenting it to Saint Macarius, the bishop of Jerusalem, for veneration by the whole world.

The icon combines the two events. Constantine, with his mother by his side, is pointing to the Cross that changed the history of the world, and Bishop Macarius, supported by two deacons, offers it for the veneration of the people. Our attention is directed to the Cross standing in the center of the icon. The building in the background shows that veneration of the Cross is something done by and for the Church.

In monasteries and cathedrals there is a special ceremony of blessing the whole world by lowering and raising the Cross. The bishop stands in the center of the church and blesses the four cardinal points of the earth, North, South, East, and West. He does so by first taking the Cross from its place on a flower-covered platform. Then, slowly bending down, he lowers it to the floor and gradually elevates it as high as he can reach. While he is performing this fourfold rite, the people repeat the invocation, "Kyrie Eleison," a hundred times. They sing more softly as the Cross is lowered and more loudly as it is raised. The Church wishes to signify by this rite that the Cross exists for the whole world and that men and women will be saved if they turn their eyes, full both of suffering and hope, toward it. Next, the people come one by one to venerate it, as a song that summarizes the whole meaning of the feast is sung: "Before thy Cross, we prostrate ourselves, O Lord, and we sing your holy Resurrection."

Whenever the Cross is celebrated—and there are two other commemorations besides that of the fourteenth of September, one on the third Sunday of Lent and the other on the first of August—the Church invites us to practice penance and to meditate on the sufferings of Christ which have brought us redemption. But with these sentiments there is always mixed a feeling of gratitude and even of jubilation.

The texts of this feast of the Cross are full of references to events reminding us that not only did loss come to the world through the wood of a tree in Eden, but also, in a figurative way, so did salvation. There is the ark of Noah, and the fact that Jacob crossed his arms to bless the sons of Joseph. Moses struck a rock with a wooden staff to make water gush forth, and he kept his arms extended despite his fatigue in order to obtain victory over Amelech. There was also the rod of Aaron.

What has just been said shows how a mere fact of experience can be made the basis of a spiritual truth we can ponder over and over again. The icon of this feast seeks to enliven us and to awaken us to the meaning of what the Church is so beautifully showing us about the one thing necessary for us.

It is worthwhile pointing out certain distinctive features in the way the Eastern Church represents the Cross on which Our Lord was crucified. Above, there is a short horizontal bar representing the inscription Pilate placed on the Cross: "Jesus of Nazareth, King of the Jews." Then there are the arms of the Cross itself, and below there is a short diagonal bar that serves as a footrest. It is higher on the right side near the good thief and sinks downward on the left side toward the unrepentant thief. This bar is the reason the Cross has been called the balance of justice, because it resembles the arms of a scale.

Every man and woman has a cross to bear. To be a disciple of Christ means taking up that cross and renouncing self (Matt 16:24). Our cross leads us where we wish to go; it points us toward God. When we willingly take up our own personal cross we are submitting ourselves to God's justice. It marks out our deviations from the true way—moments when we have cried out in rebellion against Christ who was crucified on the Cross—and moments when we have been able to say: "Remember me when you come into your kingdom." Whenever we accept the Cross, especially at the last moment of our life, we are nearest to our Lord: "This day you will be with me in Paradise."

Prayers ∾ SEPTEMBER 14

When you were raised up on the Cross, O Master, you raised up all nature, fallen through Adam.

Hail, precious Cross, guide for the blind, physician of the sick, resurrection of all who have died. You raised us when we fell into corruption. By you did corruption cease and immortality flower forth; by you have we, mortal though we are, been divinized, and the Devil defeated.

In Paradise the wood of a tree once stripped me naked. The Enemy gave me fruit to eat and thereby brought death to the world. The wood of the Cross was planted on the earth and brought to men the garment of immortality and the world was filled with joy unbounded. When we see the Cross raised up, let all of us say with one voice: Thy house is full of glory.

Today, at last, the prophecy is fulfilled, O Christ our God. We fall in worship before the place that held your feet. Embracing the tree of our salvation, we are free through the Theotokos from the passions caused by sin, O only lover of mankind.

When the tree of the cross was set in its place, O Lord, the earth shook to its foundations, and as Hades voraciously swallowed him up, so it expelled him with violent trembling. You have shown us salvation, O holy one, and so we glorify you with this refrain: Have mercy on us, O Son of God, have mercy on us.

The Exaltation of the Cross.
Mount Athos, 1999. Courtesy
of the Brothers of the Christian
Schools/De La Salle Institute.

O Lord, save your people and bless your inheritance. Give victory to those who battle evil, and with your cross protect us all.

In Paradise the tree stripped us bare, for by giving us its fruit, the enemy showed us death. But today the sight of the Cross gives joy to all the earth. For the tree that robes us all in light is raised on high. As we fall before it, O Lord, we cry out to you:

> This is the glory of your house.
> O Cross of Christ, be our strength and our protection.
> By your power make us holy,
> that we may honor you in truth and love.

O Cross of Christ, you are the hope of Christians, the guide of those who have strayed, and the haven of those tossed about by the storm of life. You are the pledge of victory for all who battle evil because you grace them with victory over every foe. For as long as they have you as their ally, they possess a weapon of peace, an unfailing trophy of victory.

Today the Cross is raised on high and all the world shares in its saving power, for you who are enthroned with the Father and the Holy Spirit have spread your arms upon it and drawn the world to know you. By your holy Cross, O Christ, enlighten us and save us.

The Presentation of the Virgin in the Temple

NOVEMBER 21

When Mary was three years old, her parents, Joachim and Anna, presented her to the high priest, Zachary, to be brought up and educated in the temple quite separate from them under the care of an angel. In doing so they were following tradition and fulfilling a vow they had made to devote to God's service the child they had long prayed for, but had received only in their old age. Thus a prophecy we find in one of the psalms had its fulfillment: "Hear, O daughter, consider and incline your ear; forget your people and your father's house" (Ps 45:11). The high point of Mary's young life was her being able to say freely from her heart: "I am the handmaid of the Lord; be it done unto me according to his word." Such a response presupposes a long spiritual preparation and this feast marks the beginning of that gradual growth to spiritual maturity. We know nothing about these years of her early life from youth to maturity, just as we lack information about Christ's early life.

In one of the texts sung at Vespers, Zachary becomes the spokesman for all humanity. He rejoices at this event without being able to say precisely why: "Here she is whom all those who have been in tribulation have been waiting for. Let Joachim rejoice and Anna leap for joy for having offered [to God] a three-year-old, the immaculate Virgin Mary. Mothers, share their joy; maidens exult; and you who are sterile join in the singing, because she has opened up for us the kingdom of heaven."

At the beginning of Advent when we look forward to the Nativity of Our Lord, the Church gives us an opportunity to meditate on her who was the docile instrument, the servant of the Lord in the birth of Christ. The news of our salvation becomes clearer and more urgent when we listen to the principal hymn of the feast: On this day the kindness of God is prefigured by the news of the salvation of all people. The theme of the feast is the fulfillment of the promises made by God, first to those of the Old Testament who lived in expectation, and then to those of the New Testament who have received the fullness of those promises. There is a constant allusion to light: "In the holy temple . . . you appear as the receiver of the inaccessible divine light."

In the icon we see the parents of Mary stretching out their hands in a gesture of offering a precious gift, the fruit of God's promise. This "holy meeting" is an anticipation of the meeting between Jesus and the holy old man, Simeon.

In the upper left, the young maiden has already embarked on her journey of preparation, of meditation. She will receive her food from the angel Gabriel. The temple with its veil prefigures the Church where God dwells. The clothes worn by Joachim and Anna harmonize with those of the Virgin. The members of the family are separating from one another, but they are not being torn apart. A gift is being peacefully offered in accordance with the will of God.

Thus it turns out that this mere legend without any historical basis has nevertheless a profound spiritual meaning for us. We too live within the inner temple of our own souls. Can we open up this temple so that Mary can be "presented" within it, so that she will agree to dwell in it, so that she can live in it and make the love for her son grow in us?

Prayers ❧ NOVEMBER 21

Today is the prelude of God's good pleasure, the herald of the salvation of all mankind. The Virgin is revealed in the temple of the Lord, thus foretelling to all the world the coming of Christ. Therefore, with all our hearts let us loudly acclaim her: Hail to you, fulfillment of the Creator's plan.

Blessed are you over all other women on earth, O Virgin Theotokos, by the Lord God most high, for he so glorified your name that your praise will never fade from the lips of men.

Today the living temple of the great king enters his temple to be groomed as his divine dwelling on earth. Let all people everywhere rejoice and be glad.

Behold the spotless temple of the Savior, his precious bridal chamber. Behold the virginal and sacred vessel of the glory of God. Today she is brought to the temple of the Most High, bearing within her the grace of the Holy Spirit. For this the angels exclaim: She is indeed the heavenly tabernacle.

A new lamp has been kindled for us, and its brilliance fills the temple of God with profound joy. For the most pure Theotokos, with her clear and shining beauty of soul, enlightens us with eternal light. Let us all entreat her today: Never let that light recede from us, O purest virgin.

The Presentation of the Virgin in the Temple. Mount Athos, 1999. Courtesy of the Brothers of the Christian Schools/ De La Salle Institute.

ΤΑ ΕΙCΟΔΙΑ ΤΗC ΘΚΥ

Christmas

This icon brings before us a variety of incidents that have come down to us either from scripture or tradition. Above, on the left, there is the journey of the Magi, and on the right an angel is announcing the news to shepherds. On the lower right, two midwives are

washing the child. This is both a rite of purification and a figure of baptism. On the left we see the temptation of Saint Joseph by Satan disguised as the god Pan clad in goat skins. He is unsuccessfully suggesting to the husband of Mary that a birth contrary to the laws of nature is impossible.

In the center is the figure of the Virgin. She is the axis around which all the other figures are arranged. The fact that she is lying on a cloth of brilliant white must be taken in a spiritual sense, signifying the fire of the Spirit, since she is also one for whom there was no room at the inn. She looks away in sorrow like a young woman who has just given birth and is concerned by what she sees must come to her son, the Lamb to be offered. The newborn child is already dressed in the swaddling clothes usually put around a corpse. He is stretched out at the base of a grave that symbolizes Sheol, the dark underworld where the dead were thought to dwell. One immediately sees the birth of God as coinciding with the low point of human suffering and hopelessness and at the same time the beginning from which new hope springs. This child, like every child who comes into the world, is born to die, but his death will be a victory over death, the triumph of life. This illumines what we read in the Gospel of John: "The light shines in the darkness and darkness has not overcome it" (or received it). Darkness will be dispersed, driven away by the light from him who by his death overcame death. From a high point in the upper center of the icon a triple-streamed ray of light descends from a circle in the sky. This is a symbol of the Father, who is impossible to represent iconographically. The whole emanation of light gives the icon the character of an epiphany and seals the involvement of the whole Trinity in the act of Incarnation performed by one Person alone.

This icon makes present to us a beginning, namely the coming of God to dwell among us, and an end, our becoming one with him. These truths are made present theologically, inasmuch as they can be talked about, and mystically, in that they enter into our heart. On a purely human plane, our sense of the mystery is heightened by the lively expressions we see on the faces of those depicted. In a broader way, the number of animals depicted shows how Christ's coming renews all creation.

The feast of Christmas was instituted in the fourth century, shortly after the Council of Nicea (325) when the Creed was formulated. The icon is a strong statement of the truth that God, in the Person of his only Son, "was born of the Virgin Mary and became man." This central idea of a God-man, of a divine Person who became man so that man could recover his own divinity, is the dominant theme sung during the liturgy, an affirmation of earth once more being joined with heaven. The Eastern Church has the sense that the birth of God on earth is a part of the whole plan of salvation, including Christ's suffering, death, and Resurrection.

In the West, the Latin Church, strongly influenced by the Franciscans, emphasizes in a fruitful way another side of the truth concerning the Incarnation: the importance of the Holy Family and of the heartwarming arrival of a long-promised little child. So, on the one hand, we are encouraged to meditate on God who has taken on flesh so that the human nature he shares can be raised to the divine. On the other hand, we are encouraged to have before our minds the moving sight of the child born in Bethlehem; our meditation will concentrate on his humanity. These are two aspects of a single reality surpassing our power to understand.

Prayers ∞ DECEMBER 25

Today is all creation filled with joy, for Christ is born of the Virgin. Your birth, O Christ our God, shines forth on the world with the light of knowledge, for those who adored the stars were taught by a star to worship you, the sun of justice, and to know you, the Orient from on high, O Lord, glory to you.

When Mary and Joseph went to register in Bethlehem as members of David's house, she was carrying the child of virginity in her womb. As the time for her delivery drew near, there was no room for them at the inn. And when a cave was shown to them, it seemed like a palace to that royal mother. So it was that Christ was born, to raise that image that fell so long ago.

Angelic choirs fill the heavens with praise of the eternal Son of the Father who has no beginning, but he has taken flesh from you in a way that defies words, O Theotokos. As the shepherds ponder this event, they are amazed by this profound mystery and they glorify God. So we, too, dare to extol you as you deserve, O Holy Lady, for it is your son who saved us.

As shepherds were spending the night playing their flutes, angelic powers suddenly appeared to them and proclaimed: Leave your campsite and your flocks. In song cry out with joy, for today is born Christ the Lord, who was pleased as God to save mankind.

The Birth of God. Mount Athos, 1999. Courtesy of the Brothers of the Christian Schools/ De La Salle Institute.

Today the Virgin gives birth to one beyond all created essences, and the earth presents a cave to this God beyond our reach. All heaven's angels join with the shepherds to sing his praises, and men of learning make their way to him with a star. For God eternal comes to all mankind as a newborn child.

Our Savior comes to us this day: The Orient of orients rises from on high in a burst of dazzling uncreated light, to dispel the darkness of our lives, that we may find the truth; for the Lord this day is born of a virgin.

He who comes forth before the dawn from his Father without a mother today comes forth from you, O Mary, without a father, and a star reveals the news to men of learning, as the shepherds join in praising your ineffable childbearing, O, full of grace.

Epiphany

JANUARY 6

The icon of the Epiphany sets before us the events surrounding the Baptism of Christ and also portrays what is said in some scriptural texts concerning the place of water in the creation of the world and as an instrument for our salvation.

Since Christ knew no sin, baptism was not conferred, as it is for us, in view of "repentance for the forgiveness of sins" (Luke 24:47).

Stepping away from the dry surface of the land, Christ immerses himself in a liquid Sheol, the place where the dead dwell. The essence of Christ's Baptism is a passage through death to resurrection, just like our baptism, as explained by Saint Paul: "Therefore we have been buried with him by baptism into death, so that, just as Christ was raised from the dead by the glory of the Father, so we too might walk in newness of life" (Rom 6:4).

What is more, Christ's entry into the Jordan brought about a true Pentecost for him personally. It was the first manifestation of the triune God. "At the baptism in the Jordan, the worship of the Trinity was manifest."

One can begin by looking vertically at the icon. Above, in the center, we see the arc of a circle breaking forth from heaven. This is the start of a theophany, God becoming manifest. The Father is present to point to the Son about whom he says: "This is my Son, the Beloved, with whom I am well pleased" (Matt 3:17). We see the triple ray of light and midway on it is the Holy Spirit in the form of a dove, bringing the love of the Father to the Son. We first hear of the dove at the beginning of Genesis when the Spirit moves over the waters at the dawn of creation, just as it does here at the dawn of the creation of a new humanity.

This baptism has meaning for all creation: "Christ is baptized; he comes forth from the water and he raises the world with him" (hymn from the Liturgy of the Day). Today the Church performs a solemn blessing of all the waters in the oceans, in rivers, and in lakes as well as of the water that is specially blessed so that the faithful can take it home and drink it on special occasions.

We can also look horizontally at the icon. Here we start with the head of Saint John the Baptist who stands in the place of all humanity. This "last of the prophets" had to force himself to baptize him "the strap of whose sandals he was not worthy to fasten" (Mark 1:17).

On the right we see the spiritual world of the angels. They are represented by three figures with veils covering their hands as a sign of adoration.

In the middle is, of course, Christ. With a gesture he blesses the watery part of the world which, seen horizontally, stands on the borders between the human and angelic worlds, and, looked at vertically, is between heaven and hell. Thus, all that composes the universe is brought together for the work of salvation.

Prayers ∽ JANUARY 6

When you were baptized in the Jordan, O Lord, the worship of the Trinity was revealed to the world, for the voice of the Father witnessed to you by calling you his beloved Son, and the Spirit, in the form of a dove, confirmed the truth of his words. O Christ our God, you have appeared to us and enlightened all the world: Glory to you.

Today the Trinity, which alone is divine, reveals itself to us in its unique, overflowing goodness. The Father speaks from the heavens as the Son is baptized, and the Holy Spirit, too, makes his presence felt. And we who perceive all this by faith cry out together: Glory to you for revealing yourself to us, O our God.

By revealing yourself to the world, you made your light shine forth on all creation. The salty sea of unbelief receded and the Jordan carried us to heaven by turning back on its course. By your lofty commandments, O Christ our God, preserve us through the prayers of the Theotokos, and save us.

Let all creation break forth in joy today at Christ's appearance in the Jordan.

Today you have appeared in the world, O Lord, and your light shines forth on us who sing your praises with understanding: You have come, you have revealed yourself to us, O inaccessible light.

Our Savior comes to us this day: In the flowing Jordan grace and truth are revealed to enlighten with brilliant light those who languish in the dark, for the light beyond our reach has appeared this day.

The Jordan is terrified by your presence and turns back in fear, while John is overcome with awe as he fulfills his prophetic ministry, and all the powers of heaven are amazed to see you baptized in that stream. Those who languish in the dark are filled with a great light and with one accord sing your praises, for you reveal yourself to the world this day, and fill all things with light.

The Epiphany. Mount Athos, 1999. Courtesy of the Brothers of the Christian Schools/ De La Salle Institute.

The Holy Meeting of the Lord

FEBRUARY 2

❧

The icon of this feast, the Holy Meeting of the Lord, is also called the Presentation of Jesus in the Temple. It illustrates the episode of Christ's life described by Saint Luke (2:21–40). Forty days after the birth of a male child (February second is precisely forty days after the feast of Christmas), Jewish parents were obliged by the Law (Lev 12:2–8) to present their newborn sons in the temple and to offer a sacrifice—"a pair of turtle doves or two young pigeons."

Joseph and Mary are received by the old man Simeon, a just and pious man, who was "looking forward to the consolation of Israel." God had assured him that he would not die before he had seen Christ the Savior (Luke 2:26). In the icon we see behind Simeon the prophetess Anna, who had been serving God night and day in the temple.

Simeon and Anna had lived in expectation of the Messiah. They represent the fullness of time, that peaceful fullness where men and women stand confidently in God's everlasting peace.

"Master, now you are dismissing your servant in peace, for my eyes have seen your salvation . . . "

This is the icon of the Holy Meeting, where Simeon meets the Messiah, where the Old Testament meets the New. The four adults seen in the icon are all prayerfully performing actions prescribed by the ritual of the law. Christ awaits as expectations come to fulfillment and promises become reality. The old man holds in his own hands the child of promise; there is nothing left for him to do except die in peace.

In the background we see the temple. The event presented by this icon is fundamental to the existence of the Church. It shows the Church at the turning point between it and the synagogue as a place where sacrifice is offered and God is worshiped both symbolically and in fact.

The old rite of sacrificing turtle doves now gives place to an action with another meaning, the consecration of a child for the service of God. In this sense the presentation of a child in the temple is still alive within the Orthodox Church. For Christ, this consecration will reach its highest point when he himself is offered as a sacrifice, a Lamb offered up.

Enhanced by his foreknowledge of the greatness of the one he holds in his arms, Simeon speaks prophetically to Mary: Your son will be a sign that provokes contradiction, and a sword will pierce your own spirit. He reminds us of the fulfillment of all prophecies: Israel has been delivered.

Prayers ∽ FEBRUARY 2

Rejoice, O full of grace, O Theotokos and maiden pure, for from you there arose the sun of justice, Christ our God, who enlightens those in darkness. You, too, exult and be glad, just and aged Simeon, for you bore in your arms the savior and redeemer of our souls, and from him have we all received the grace of resurrection.

On Mount Sinai, Moses saw the back of God, and he heard God's voice as a storm raging in the darkness around him. This same God took flesh without change, and now Simeon has taken him into his arms. For the old man, life is now complete, and so he prepares joyfully to depart this life, saying: Now you may let your servant go in peace, Master, as you said you would.

The eternal word of the Father appeared in the flesh to all mankind and submits today to the law of which he is the author. Have mercy on us, O Lord, and save us.

For man's salvation you took flesh of Mary and sanctified her maiden womb, and with yourself you blessed the aged Simeon by resting in his arms. Now that you have saved us, O Christ our God, in these troubled times give your lasting peace, and for all those whom you hold dear provide strong, undaunted faith, O only lover of mankind.

The Presentation in the Temple. Fifteenth-century Byzantine icon. Tretyakov Gallery, Moscow, Russia. Courtesy of Scala/Art Resource, NY.

Led to the temple by the Holy Spirit, the elder took into his arms the master of the entire universe, and in his joy he cried out for all to hear: Now you may let your servant go in peace, Master, for my eyes have seen the salvation you prepared as a light for the nations and the glory of your people Israel.

The prophetess had taken to spending all her time in the temple in prayer, and the old man kept praying to be released from the bonds of this life. When finally he held in his arms the creator of all and found his release, the two old people rejoiced and prepared for eternal life.

The Annunciation

MARCH 25

❦

The manner chosen by Saint Luke to tell the story of the Annunciation is at the same time ethereal and weighty (Luke 1:26–38). The icon before our eyes conveys every nuance of that story in admirable detail. The hymns for this feast skillfully serve the same purpose. Painting and poetry intertwined reveal to us what the Church intends for us to understand during the course of this feast.

What is striking about this icon is the equilibrium of power between the three figures in it and their harmonious relation to one another. One becomes aware of a triangle with the Virgin as its apogee and the angel and the dove as opposite points that nevertheless converge on her.

The dove, enclosed by a triple set of rays, descends from a break in the heavens, which allows us to think of the Father present in all his infinite power. Thus, it is clear that the three Persons of the Trinity all play an active role in the Incarnation.

We see the angel Gabriel as an expansive figure hastening forward to deliver a message from the one who sent him. He has a pilgrim's staff in his hand. The flowing pleats of his great mantle mirror the downward sweep of his wings. All this is in keeping with someone aware of the importance of his mission. He speaks for God when he begins by saying, "Hail Mary, full of grace, the Lord is with you."

His arm extended toward Mary helps convey God's message to the mind of Mary, who needs to be reassured and encouraged: "Fear not, Mary, for you have found grace before God." The angel carries a blessing to her.

The Virgin, motionless and graceful, is seated. Though her face has the easily understandable concern Luke ascribes to her, there is in her bearing a trustful acceptance that is free of worry. We are at a solemn moment when the mighty "Let it be done" is about to be spoken. "Behold the handmaid of the Lord. Let it be done unto me according to thy word"—crucial words in the history of humanity. In answer to this acceptance there is a corresponding response from God, the sending forth of the Holy Spirit. It is to be noted that the divine action comes only in response to the prior assent of a woman. Thus history becomes the story of our salvation.

We see Mary seated inside the temple where, according to tradition, she has been spending her life prayerfully in solitary preparation for her role in God's plan. In her hand she holds the distaff, a cleft stick about three yards long used for winding yarn in preparation for spinning a new veil for the temple. The overhanging veil has its own deep meaning, as one of the hymns of the feast reminds us:

"Today is revealed an eternal mystery: The Son of God becomes the son of man."

Prayers ∞ MARCH 25

Today is the crown of our salvation, and a mystery hidden from eternity is now made known: God's son becomes the virgin's son, and a prince of heaven's hosts proclaims the grace of this good news. Therefore, with him let us greet the maid and say: Rejoice, O full of grace, the Lord is with you.

Today the Word of the Lord descends to this earth, and the angel stands before the maiden and exclaims: Of all women you are the most blessed, for your virginity alone has pleased the Most High. Now, without disturbing it, he makes you the mother of the eternal Word and Lord, God himself who will save the world from error.

Today, the condemnation of Eve is lifted through you, O Theotokos, and the debt of that first woman is paid in full. Obtain for us, as well, O Holy Lady, the full remission of our sins.

To you, victorious Lady, we your servants inscribe this hymn of thanks, for you have rescued us from tribulation. With your power that never fails, preserve us our whole life long from every evil, that we may ever sing: Hail to you, O bride and maiden undefiled.

The sun that sheds its light on all the earth cannot compare with you, O Holy Virgin, for you are a glowing sanctuary of the divine sun, a lamp wherein the first light of heaven dwelled. By your prayers, O Theotokos, obtain for us a share in the light of wisdom and understanding, and save us.

O leader of the hosts of heaven, you are the glorious servant and minister of the divine Trinity, that most radiant and ineffable mystery, that awesome and almighty author of everything that is. Pray without ceasing for us all, that, spared all sorrows and trouble, we may ever hail you as our great protector.

The Annunciation. Fourteenth-century Byzantine icon. Icon Gallery, Ohrid, Macedonia. Courtesy of Erich Lessing/Art Resource, NY.

The Entry into Jerusalem

SIXTH SUNDAY OF LENT

❧

Before undergoing his Passion, Christ, for the only time in his life, is acclaimed at the gates of Jerusalem as the Son of David, that is, as a descendant of the royal family of the Hebrew people. The people acclaim him and put before him symbols that belong to a Messiah King. Clothes are spread beneath the feet of the young donkey on which he rides. Palm branches—signs of victory—are waved before him as are olive branches, signs of peace and anointing. All this is accompanied by the joyful welcoming cry "Hosanna."

In this icon we see Christ's power over an enthusiastic crowd bent on showing their admiration for him in a public manner. If we look closely, we can discern two aspects of this feast: a kingly power never exercised by Christ but acknowledged by the people through evident signs, and the deep humility that guides Christ himself. The Messiah is not riding on a horse—the symbol of a king going forth to war or bent on conquest—but instead on the colt of an ass, as Zechariah had prophesied, echoing Isaiah's description of the suffering servant.

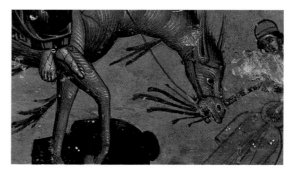

When we see the king entering the earthly Jerusalem for the first time in conformity with the will of the Father, we are led to think of the Second Coming in glory into the heavenly Jerusalem where he will henceforth rule for ever.

If we look at this icon horizontally, we see three groups of figures in the lower range. Above each group there is something else that deserves our attention. At the higher level on the left there is Mount Golgotha and in the center there is a tree (which often symbolizes the Cross). At the higher level on the right is the city of Jerusalem, an enclosed place that has shut its gates on Jesus. Below on the left are the disciples, and on the right the people of Jerusalem ready to receive the prophet. Christ is in the center, blessing both groups and thereby uniting them. Two perspectives emerge for us from the icon: we see Christ's entry into the city of Jerusalem as a prelude to his death with all its consequences for the world, and we see an enthusiastic crowd carrying palm branches, with children spreading clothes under the feet of the donkey like we do today when we spread a red carpet for a head of state to walk on.

In the Byzantine liturgy the acclamation, "Blessed is he who comes in the name of the Lord" is still sung just before Communion and helps us see that the Eucharist is already a prelude to our entry into the heavenly Jerusalem.

Christ's entry into Jerusalem just before his going up to Golgotha and his descent into hell is celebrated with seriousness but also with a special joy. The Jewish children wave palm branches and cry out "Hosanna," proclaiming the forthcoming victory over death. "The Hebrew children, predicting the victory of the Resurrection, went before you with tree branches and palms" (Vespers). The principal hymn of the feast (Troparion) reminds us of meaning of Palm Sunday for our life: "Buried with you in Baptism, O Christ our God, we have been deemed worthy of immortal life thanks to your Resurrection, and we cry out this hymn of praise: Hosanna in the highest; blessed is he who comes in the name of the Lord!"

Prayers ✒ SIXTH SUNDAY OF LENT

Today the grace of the Holy Spirit gathers us together, and lifting your Cross on high, we cry aloud: Blessed in the Lord's name is he who comes! Hosanna in the highest.

Here he is, O Zion! Here is your king, gentle and meek, coming forth to confront his enemies in humility and without resentment. Rejoice then, O Zion, holy city! With great rejoicing take up your palms and branches, and go forth to meet him with this joyful cry: Hosanna in the highest.

Today the Son and Word of God the Father, like him without beginning and eternal, enters Jerusalem seated on the colt of an ass. The cherubim know better than to gaze on him, yet the children run before him with their palms and branches and they sing to him this mystic hymn of praise: Blessed is he who comes to save us! Hosanna in the highest.

People everywhere! All you nations! Everyone, come forth! Behold the king of heaven as he enters Jerusalem, the holy city, seated on the colt of an ass as if on a lofty throne. Come, behold him whom Isaiah once saw; behold the bridegroom of the new Zion, for he comes in the flesh to save us from our sins. And to celebrate his pure and undefiled nuptials, the innocent children gather to sing his praises, and so with them we also greet him, exclaiming: To him who grants great mercy, Hosanna in the highest.

Christ's Entry into Jerusalem.
Sixteenth-century icon.
Museum of Macedonia,
Skopje, Macedonia. Courtesy
of Scala/Art Resource, NY.

Rejoice, O city of Zion, and be glad! You too, exult, O Church of the Lord. For behold your king comes to you seated on a beast of burden and acclaimed by your youth. You, too, go forth to meet him, crying out to him and singing: Blessed is he who shows mercy to us, Hosanna in the highest!

To assure us, before you suffered, of our own resurrection, you raised Lazarus from the dead, Christ, our God. So we, too, acclaim you with victory branches, as we hail you for your triumph over death. Hosanna in the highest! Blessed is he who comes in the name of the Lord.

At first they sang in praise of Christ our God, waving their palms and branches in welcome, but later, some ungrateful among these people would seize him and crucify him. As for us, with faith that never wavers, let us acclaim him as our benefactor, unceasingly hailing him with this refrain: Blessed are you for coming to ransom Adam!

The Resurrection

EASTER SUNDAY

❧

There are two ways in which icon painters depict the event this feast celebrates. One derives from the gospel account (Mark 16:1–11) and shows an angel announcing Christ's Resurrection to women gathered at the tomb. The other, seen in the icon presented here, shows Christ's descent into the depths of hell where the dead are imprisoned and where he fulfills his divine and human mission on earth by overcoming the forces of evil.

We have already seen light penetrating through darkness in the icons for Christmas and the Epiphany. They too direct our gaze toward the central combat against evil continually waged by Christ during his life on earth. In this picture we see him winning his final and decisive struggle against the enemy.

The figure of Christ shines forth with full divine power against an oval shaped geometric figure called the mandorla (a Greek word meaning "almond" and therefore descriptive of the shape of the figure we see). This figure also appears in the icons of the Transfiguration and the Dormition. It suggests the existence of a strength and a power beyond anything we

know. This higher force encompasses all below; heaven penetrates the earth. In the Easter icon the most distant realms—heaven and hell— touch one another. Between them stand the souls of the dead.

In the upper part of the icon is the Cross, standing between two angels. On it Christ suffered and by it he broke the gates of hell. No one can hope to rise again without bearing the cross as long as he or she still lives here below.

Like lightning, Christ plunges into the nether world and shatters it with whirlwind force. We see this in the upward movement of his trailing garments. (We can see similar movement in Gabriel's cloak in the icon of the Annunciation). The surging power of Christ's Resurrection does not move upward from below but rather downward from above. It bursts forth at the lowest point of the Son of God's self-abasement. "You came down to earth to save Adam, and when you did not find him you sent as far as hell to seek him" (Matins of Holy Saturday).

The Easter hymn joyfully sings: "Christ is risen from the dead." This is no metaphor.

Christ did not emerge from the grave alone. Together with himself, he lifts all humanity, beginning with those who lived earliest. He first visited Adam and Eve, whom we see kneeling in the foreground of the icon. Christ stretches out his hand toward them to help them emerge from the nether world. The old Adam and the new meet face to face. Following Adam is the whole procession of his descendants. They prefigure the shining host of those who will follow the new Adam. On the left side

we see King David, King Solomon, and Moses; on the right are the three prophets.

Beneath Christ's feet are the shattered gates of hell and their broken bars and hinges. "By death Christ conquers death." Saint Peter alludes to this destruction of death's power: "God raised him up, having freed him from death, because it was impossible for him to be held in its power" (Acts 2:24).

After Christ's descent into hell there remains no place in the whole universe where God's light has not shone, nor any spot, however remote, that he has not visited. This is true both of the land where the dead dwell and the interior hell where some people spend their lives.

Once more it is Saint Peter who speaks of the hope now alive everywhere: "For this is the reason the gospel was proclaimed even to the dead, so that, though they had been judged in the flesh as everyone is judged, they might live in the spirit as God does" (1 Pet 4:6). There are no longer any prisoners: "He has given life to those in the tomb."

Prayers ∽ EASTER SUNDAY

Christ is risen from the dead, conquering death by death, and bestowing life on those in the grave.

We have seen Christ's resurrection! In adoration let us fall before the holy Lord Jesus, for he alone has never sinned! Your Cross, O Christ, do we honor and we glorify your Resurrection! For you alone are really God: Your name is ever on our lips! Let us fall down in worship; let us adore his third-day rising from the dead. Through his Cross, joy has filled the world. A blessing for the Lord be ever on our lips; the praise and glory of his rising ever be our song. By bearing all the sufferings of the Cross, a death blow has he dealt to death.

Come, let us all go forth to meet him! Let us welcome our triumphant Christ! Today he bursts the tomb in glory, God's own pasch, our soul's salvation! With heaven's powers let us celebrate this greatest of all festivals, filled with joy and gladness.

Although you went into the grave, Immortal One, you destroyed the power of hell. You arose a mighty victor, Christ our God, bringing peace to your apostles, joy for myrrh-bearing men, and resurrection for the fallen.

Shine forth in splendor, new Jerusalem! The Lord's bright glory bursts upon you! Skip for joy in happy festival, O Zion! And you, O purest one! Rejoice with us O Theotokos, for Christ your Son has risen!

An angel greeted you, O full of grace; O purest Virgin, rejoice! And again I say rejoice! For your Son has risen from the grave, and with himself has raised the dead. People everywhere, rejoice. O day of resurrection! Let us beam with God's own pride! Let everyone embrace in joy! Let us warmly greet those we meet and treat them all like brothers and sisters, even those who hate us. For in his rising is all grace and pardon! Let all the earth resound with this song: Christ is risen from the dead, conquering death by death and bestowing life on those in the grave.

The Descent of the Holy Spirit.
Seventeenth-century icon.
Museum of History,
Moscow, Russia. Courtesy of
Beniaminson/Art Resource, NY.

The Ascension

ASCENSION THURSDAY

*L*ooked at vertically, this icon is organized around the Virgin with two angels in white below, while above Christ is seated with his right hand extended in blessing. On the lower right and left sides the disciples are agitatedly looking upward; some are stretching forth their arms. The wings of the angels form an upside-down triangle whose vertex is on earth. The movement within the whole icon is an upward motion stretching out laterally toward the infinite. Christ's Ascension defines this impetus toward infinity.

Looked at horizontally, the icon presents two levels, one in heaven and the other on earth. Heaven is to be thought of as something interior rather than cosmic. Christ is here depicted against an oval shaped, green colored mandorla or aura of glory. The mandorla is an inner space where Christ reigns. Heaven and earth are both separated and united, as a text of Matins says: "Christ, having raised the race of Adam from the hellish prison where it lay in humiliation, has by his Ascension raised it to heaven." The unity of these two realms is suggested by the repetition of the colors in the

robes of the angels here, and there in the clothes of the apostles.

Theological truths found in this icon are very rich. The angels who hold up the mandorla are also opening up the gates of heaven. We hear of these gates in Psalm 24: "Lift up your heads, O gates! and be lifted up, O ancient doors! that the King of glory may come in. Who is the King of glory? The LORD, strong and mighty."

In one hand Christ holds the scroll of the word and with the other hand he blesses his disciples (Luke 24:50) and promises to send them the Holy Spirit: "The Lord has ascended to heaven to send the Consoler to the world," as one of the texts for this feast expresses it. The Ascension is the necessary link between Easter and Pentecost. It brings to a close Christ's life on earth and is a preparation for the coming of the Spirit who will bring life to the time from Pentecost to the Second Coming.

In the center of the icon are two angels dressed in white. The brightness of the colors enveloping them makes them stand out from all the other figures and gives them an unmis-

takable importance. Indeed, the Acts of the Apostles tell us that two angels in white instruct the apostles not to look any longer up to heaven but to turn their attention to the earth. This is a hard lesson, but not a sad one, even though it involves separation from the Master whom they love. As we learn, "They returned to Jerusalem with great joy and were continually in the temple blessing God."

Prayers ∾ ASCENSION THURSDAY

Almighty Lord and Father, author of wonders beyond our power to grasp: This evening, like those men of Galilee, we, too, stand before you with uplifted minds and hearts, contemplating your Son's Ascension in glory. As we celebrate this feast of his return to your hand, we pray you to let his light dispel the darkness of our ignorance and illumine our way to greater faith and wisdom. Make us worthy of the perfection he won for us by his unique offering of himself, for, just as he, our head, preceded us in glory, so do we, his body, also hope to follow.

For blest and glorified is your most honorable and magnificent name, Father, Son, and Holy Spirit, now and forever, and unto ages of ages.

The Ascension. Mount Athos, 1999. Courtesy of the Brothers of the Christian Schools/ De La Salle Institute.

Pentecost

SECOND SUNDAY AFTER THE ASCENSION

❦

❧ Behold we celebrate the feast of Pentecost, the coming of the Holy Spirit, the fulfillment of promises and of our hope.   —*Text of Vespers*

This is amongst the greatest of all feasts and in it the revelation of the Holy Trinity is complete. God manifests himself and the Holy Spirit descends on the apostles—and on all men and women—with a profusion of supernatural gifts. As a sign that the liturgical year has come to its fullness, all the Sundays up to the Great Lent will be numbered as Sundays after Pentecost.

For Christ, John the Baptist was the precursor, just as Christ is for the Holy Spirit: "The Word became flesh so that men might receive the Holy Spirit" (Saint Athanasius). At the Baptism in the Jordan, God's presence is manifest by the hovering of the dove over the humanity of the son and by the voice of the Father proclaiming Christ's divine sonship. At Pentecost, the Holy Spirit is born to all people, each one personally, by the mediation of tongues of fire, and he adopts them so that through the gift of tongues men and women will be able to announce the Word, Immortal God and Savior, that "having been illumined they may be able to reveal heaven" (Matins).

The Church has its firm beginning in this outpouring of gifts: "The Holy Spirit is the giver of all good things; from him as from a mighty spring prophecy flows; he consecrates priests; he teaches wisdom to the illiterate; he makes theologians out of fishermen; he gives form to the whole Church" (Great Vespers).

High up in the center of the icon there is a semicircular opening in the heavens. From it fire comes forth. The same fire comes for all, but there is an individual and personal tongue of fire for each person. Within the Church there is thus a solution for the problem of what is personal and what is communal, of what is of the individual and what is of society. Christ assumes all humanity in the unity of his body, and the Holy Spirit adapts specially for each man and woman the graces and charisms he gives them.

The liturgical texts for this feast speak of the marvelous possibility that our language can again be unified. It was divided because of the arrogant plan of building the tower of Babel as high as the heavens. Ever since, our languages have been a source of division among us. Tongues of fire rested on each of the apostles. Immediately they spoke foreign languages and, what is more, they "told the marvels of God." The gifts of the Holy Spirit not only loosen tongues but also allow every spirit to commune with spirit.

Saint Paul speaks of various gifts: wisdom, the power to cure, prophecy, discernment of spirits, speaking in tongues (1 Cor 12). These gifts attain their fullness in the saints. Icon painters strive to convey this radiation of spiritual light, this transfiguration a saint receives. The background of an icon is often layered with subtle shades of gold. It is frequently spoken of as spirit because it is a somewhat hidden source from which light radiates. We find here an underlying resource of the painter's art.

The kind of platform on which the apostles are sitting high above the world represents

the upper room. The Church is caught between two contradictory attitudes—one that seeks an inward concentration centered on God and the other open to the whole world on which heavenly gifts must be spread. The semicircular arc in the upper part of the icon is open upward to inspire the world of darkness so that it can be brought to the light. Thus there is a promise of salvation for those who are captives "in darkness and the shadow of death." That was the mighty task assigned to the Church on the day of its foundation.

Prayers ∽ SECOND SUNDAY AFTER THE ASCENSION

O Holy Trinity, eternal being transcending time and human comprehension; O you who are knowledge that has never been taught, wisdom that has never been learned or acquired; O uncreated nature beyond all change, unfathomable being, Father, Son, and Holy Spirit: As we celebrate the wonder that thundered forth upon the world at the third hour of that unique and singular day, we beseech your graciousness: send down upon us that cherished breeze, the long-desired and prayed-for Spirit. Let his divinity purge us of all that is base and unworthy, and burn away every polluting evil from our lives. Let him fortify our justice and honesty and give us the wisdom to stand before you in awe and wonder at all times, that, before we return to the earth we came from, we may return to you, our only God and Savior.

For yours it is to have mercy on us and save us, O God, and we give you glory, Father, Son, and Holy Spirit, now and forever, and unto ages of ages.

O Lord Jesus Christ, our God! You have given us your peace and bestowed on us the gift of your Holy Spirit, and as you continue to remain with us throughout life, you grace the faithful with an inheritance that shall not be taken away. Today, in a vivid manner, you gave your apostles this grace, placing on their lips those fiery tongues so that, through them, we, together with the whole human race, have received the knowledge of God into our hears through our own language.

The Feast of Pentecost. Mount Athos, 1999. Courtesy of the Brothers of the Christian Schools/De La Salle Institute.

We are enlightened by the very light of the Holy Spirit, who through those fiery tongues delivered us from falsehood and deception as from darkness itself. By their energy we have been made disciples of the faith, praising you together with your Father and Holy Spirit, one divinity, one power, and one authority.

You are the radiance of the Father, O Christ, the unchanging and immutable image of his essence and nature, the very wellspring of all wisdom and grace. Give us understanding, Lord. Open our sinful lips and teach us how and what to pray for, for though the enormity of our wrongdoing is beyond description, you know that your loving kindness is more than enough to blot it out completely. Look at us. We kneel here before you, filled with an overwhelming awe and reverence for you, and we cast our despair into the ocean of your compassion. Guide our feet along your paths, for you govern and sustain all creation with the power of your wisdom. Yes, show us the path to walk, O tranquil haven of those in turmoil. Let our deliberations reflect your wisdom. Dispel our ignorance by the understanding that comes from you. Make all our actions reflect the awe and reverence you deserve. Create within us a new and constant spirit. Bring stability to our stumbling, vacillating minds and hearts by the power of your sovereign Spirit, that we may be worthy of doing your will and attaining salvation. Give us a constant awareness of your presence, that we may live each day with the vision of your glorious coming ever before our eyes. Protect us from the things of this world that would corrupt us, and strengthen us with the hope of the happiness of the age to come.

Your yourself said, Master, that whatever we ask in your name, we will receive unconditionally from your Father, the co-eternal God. Therefore, on this feast of the descent of the Holy Spirit, we sinners ask you to grant us, in your goodness, all that we need for salvation. For you are indeed the generous giver of all that is good, providing graciously for all our needs. You are the compassionate one, the merciful one, who shared our nature without being touched by our sinfulness, becoming yourself a sacrifice for our sins.

Be gracious to us, then, O Lord. Hear us from your divine dwelling and make us holy. Shelter us with your mercy and love and do not turn away from us. We have sinned, indeed, O Lord, but we serve you alone. We adore no other, nor do we lift our hands in praise of any other. Pardon us all our sins and accept this prayer we make to you today on bended knee. Receive it as a fragrant perfume of incense rising before your throne and welcome it into your glorious kingdom.

For you are a merciful and loving God, and we give you glory, Father, Son, and Holy Spirit, now and forever, and unto ages of ages.

The Transfiguration

AUGUST 6

⁂

This icon sets before us the story told by all three synoptic writers about the time when Christ took three of his disciples, Peter, James, and John, to Mount Tabor and was transfigured before them. All of a sudden they saw him above them dressed in dazzling white garments. The eyes of these three men, sinners like ourselves, and accustomed like we are to the darkness of this world, were for a moment transformed so that they could see the "uncreated" light of the Spirit, the vision of the divine energies.

In a certain way it was really the apostles who were transfigured; it was they who became able to see. For them the experience was upsetting, even unbearable, as we see by the positions of their bodies. At least two of them look as if they had been subjected to physical violence. They are on the ground with their faces hidden as if to protect their sight.

In sharp contrast to the figures in the lower part of the icon, we see Christ standing straight and motionless. Serenity emanates from him as he converses with two great men of the Old Testament, Moses and Elijah.

The notion of "uncreated light" appears throughout the Old Testament. For instance, when Moses came down from the mountain where he had been speaking with God for forty days (Exod 34:28–30), his face shone so brilliantly that the Hebrews were struck with fear (Exod 34:30). Elijah heard God speak to him in the still, small sound of a breeze (1 Kgs 19:13) and was carried off in a fiery chariot. These two representatives, one of the law and the other of the prophets, are conversing with Christ on his departure for Jerusalem, his Passion. The fact of Christ's glory cannot be separated from that other formidable fact. One comes to glory only through the Cross.

The voice of the Father makes itself heard here, just as it did when Christ was baptized in the Jordan: "This is my beloved Son in whom I am well pleased. Listen to him." These words show that supernatural graces—Christ's glory, for instance, or the sight of uncreated light—are not isolated facts; they are given only when there is obedience, the will to be conformed to the will of the Father. The Transfiguration can also be seen as a consolation given to Christ before he climbs the mountain of Golgotha and to the apostles soon to be tempted by despair when they see the beloved Master threatened by death. Such graces are also given to any man or woman in times of trial.

The first meaning of the Transfiguration, then, is the glorification of the Son by the Father before the final degradation. It is a glorious manifestation of the Trinity: the voice of the Father, the luminous cloud, and the Son, all three in an intimate unity.

The Transfiguration affects every person, living or dead: "On this day on Mount Tabor Christ has transformed Adam's darkened nature; having covered him with his glory he divinizes him" (Vespers).

It is even true to say that the whole universe is transformed by this glorious event. Saint Paul says the world "groans and suffers the pains of childbirth," but the sun that enlightens the world will not fail to set. "Christ shining in glory on the mountain floods the world with light" (Vespers).

This is the preeminent light-giving icon. It is good for us to look at it and meditate on it in moments of great pain.

Prayers ∽ AUGUST 6

How many times since our youth, Lord, have we begged for your mercy, only to go on taking it for granted! Unlike the prophet David, we have failed to attain repentance. During these days when we celebrate the Transfiguration of your Son, we implore you to bathe us in his light, that we may understand repentance and persevere in our pursuit of it. We beg you, O God: With this feast, make us cleaner than spring water; wash us, and make us whiter than snow.

By the grace and mercy and love for us of your only Son, with whom you are blest, together with your all-holy, good, and life-giving Spirit, now and forever, and unto ages of ages.

The Transfiguration. Mount Athos, 1999. Courtesy of the Brothers of the Christian Schools/De La Salle Institute.

The Dormition

AUGUST 15

❧❦❧

Tradition is the only basis for this feast. No gospel text alludes to the circumstances that surrounded the departure of the Holy Virgin from this world. Saint John Damascene records what tradition from the earliest ages of Christianity has to say about her death. The apostles were dispersed to the four corners of the earth when Mary, who was dwelling with Saint John the Evangelist in Jerusalem, felt her strength failing and expressed the desire to see the twelve beside her once more. The twelve apostles are here present at the last moments of her who had been "the temple of God" and to see her son come to carry away his mother's soul. She was buried near Gethsemane.

It turned out that Saint Thomas again arrived late and asked to look one more time on the face of her who had brought forth the Savior. They went to her tomb, opened it, and found it empty. Mary then appeared and confirmed the fact of her bodily Assumption.

This icon matches the icon of the Ascension. There, angels clear the way for the Son of God; here, the Son of God himself comes to carry off the woman who brought him into the world. The dominant idea here, as in the Ascension, is the unity of earth and heaven: "In your Dormition, O Mother of God, you did not leave the world." Mary remains attentive to what happens in the world, and she does not cease to intercede for it.

The horizontal axis of this icon passes through the body of Mary. On both sides of Mary's body the grieving disciples cling to her funeral bed. Several saints with their heads bowed in sadness join with them. They are absorbed in meditation as their serious faces attest. The liturgical texts for the day sometimes express a certain sadness and sometimes are full of hope: "Your death was a passage to a better and everlasting life, Lady most pure; it carried you from mortality to what is truly lasting and divine, Immaculate Virgin, to contemplate your Son and Savior in joy" (Matins).

In this icon Christ is shown as a grown man carrying the child-sized soul of his mother.

This scene is the counterpart of the icons that show Mary as mother holding the child Jesus in her arms. The relative size of each figure is inverted. Mary as Christ's mother gives him earthly life; Christ helps his mother pass beyond the frontiers of that life: "You have been carried into life, you who are the Mother of Life."

The presence of the twelve apostles and of the angels shows how highly the Church honors the Mother of God. This feast is striking because it symbolizes the hope of salvation now open to all humanity: "The most holy Assumption of the Virgin Mother of God brings the heavenly powers to rejoice with us on earth as we honor you in song: Blessed are you, O God."

Prayers ∽ AUGUST 15

In giving birth, your conception was without seed, and in falling asleep, your death was without corruption. A second wonder followed the first, O Theotokos, for how could a girl untouched by man nurse a child while still a virgin? And how were you embalmed and buried as dead, only to pass body and soul into the world to come? Hail, full of grace.

In prayer, watchful and constant is she at all times, and all who seek her help are soon consoled by her unfailing aid. Neither death nor tomb overcame her, for, as Mother of Christ the Light, she was taken into life by that very one who deigned to dwell in her ever-maiden womb.

PART TWO

Icons in Prayer

Notes on the Icon of the Trinity

❧

Rublev's icon of the Trinity is one of the most beautiful of all icons. It is well known even in the West.

It is easy to think that meditation on the theological truths contained in this icon has power to bring about the union of all Christians. The subtle beauty hidden within it draws our minds and our hearts to the love of the triune God from whom comes all the good in the world.

The story of Abraham's hospitality to three strangers (Gen 18) is well known. In the icon we see that the three persons represented are travelers because of the staffs they have in their hands. Tradition predating Rublev chose to see in these visitors an intimation of the not-yet-revealed intimate nature of God, one in three Persons.

What led several Church Fathers to see in this story of the three visitors to Abraham an allegory about the Trinity? The early Greek Fathers noticed the language Abraham uses when he addresses the visitors a second time. He addresses them at first as if they were three

and next as if they were only one. The way the words are used is, to say the least, striking.

Abraham and Sarah busily set up a table and offer a meal to their guests. Under those circumstances and on that very day, the Lord promises the aged couple that they will have a son, Isaac. We know that later, when it comes time for Abraham to offer a sacrifice to God, his fidelity will be tried. He will be asked to sacrifice his firstborn son.

Every aspect of this story is of prime importance in God's plan of redemption for humanity. One cannot fail to be amazed that at the very beginning of those events that would change history, the first thing we see is a human being, Abraham, offering hospitality to God (in the person of three strangers). He shows the same willingness here as he will show later when he is asked to offer his son in sacrifice. When a man shows himself capable of such gestures, is it not suitable that God should choose to multiply a hundredfold the meaning of those gestures? Will he not lend them a more than natural meaning?

Rublev gives us only the essentials. All superfluous details have been eliminated so that nothing interferes with the story he has to tell. The meal is reduced to a cup (a figure of the Eucharist) standing on a white tablecloth. The table is positioned above a space where a rectangular figure has been drawn. The four corners of this rectangle stand for the four corners of the universe to which God's mercy extends.

The three angels are gathered for what texts of the liturgy refer to as the Great Council. In it the unparalleled decision was made to send the Son from heaven down to earth. He is represented by the angel on the left. The eyes of the two others are turned toward him. His attitude is one of humble acceptance. The Holy Spirit is represented by the angel on the right. His hand traces out the image of a dove with its wings poised to descend. The angel in the center represents the Father in all his might. Two of his fingers are extended to signify the double nature—divine and human—of the Son who will bind together heaven and earth.

What is before us is the solemn moment when Christ willingly takes on himself the sacrifice on which the salvation of all the world depends. God can do nothing without us; he respects our liberty. He found in Abraham a just man who responded to what was asked of him. Here God's will and the will of a man come together in the deepest harmony. Here we have the ground of the old alliance between God and humanity. None of our discordant acts, our wandering off the track or our misdeeds, will terminate this bond between God and us. The mercy of God is unlimited. The old alliance will subsist and become the figure of the new.

In the middle of the fourteenth century, Saint Serge of Radonezh founded a famous monastery which he dedicated to the Holy Trinity. Some twenty years after the saint's death, Rublev painted the icon of the Trinity as part of the icon-screen of the monastery church. The people in the surrounding country were at that time undergoing great suffering because of the barbarism of cruel Tartars. On every side people lived in the greatest misery and ignorance. These two men, the founder and the artist, one by his determination to establish a monastery and the other by his power to paint in ethereal colors, spread an understanding of the Trinity that has never been surpassed. Through these two great men, the love of one God in three Persons spread from churches to homes and into the hearts of men and women. The spiritual energies of the Russian church shone forth not in abstract theological speculations but in the contemplation of the central mystery of God's love.

Wolves wandered everywhere in those northern forests, but the thought of what is deepest about God permeated people's minds. The mystery as represented by Rublev had a profound influence because the image he succeeded in making spoke so clearly to all. In later years, other painters with slight variations helped to spread throughout Russia a deep sense of the life-giving doctrine of the Holy Trinity.

This majestic and peaceful icon vibrates with joy before all men and women as a source of happiness and as the effective model of all human love. A community of all humanity thus becomes possible. It has as its source an inner power from God, who from the moment of creation willed that unity in all its reflected splendor.

Many writers have spoken of the symbolism and the aesthetic qualities of this icon. For the moment it will be sufficient to call attention to the vitality and dynamism of the movement one can see if one draws a circle (1) beginning with the foot of the angel on the right up to the mountain where there stands a tree (which evokes the wood of the Cross because it has its roots within the axis of the chalice), (2) continuing in a curve that passes from the central angel to the angel on the left who is upright and motionless, and (3) terminating where it began in an unending circular movement. Three sides of the table set by Abraham are occupied, but the fourth side remains open to all those who want to come to the banquet offered to us by God's love.

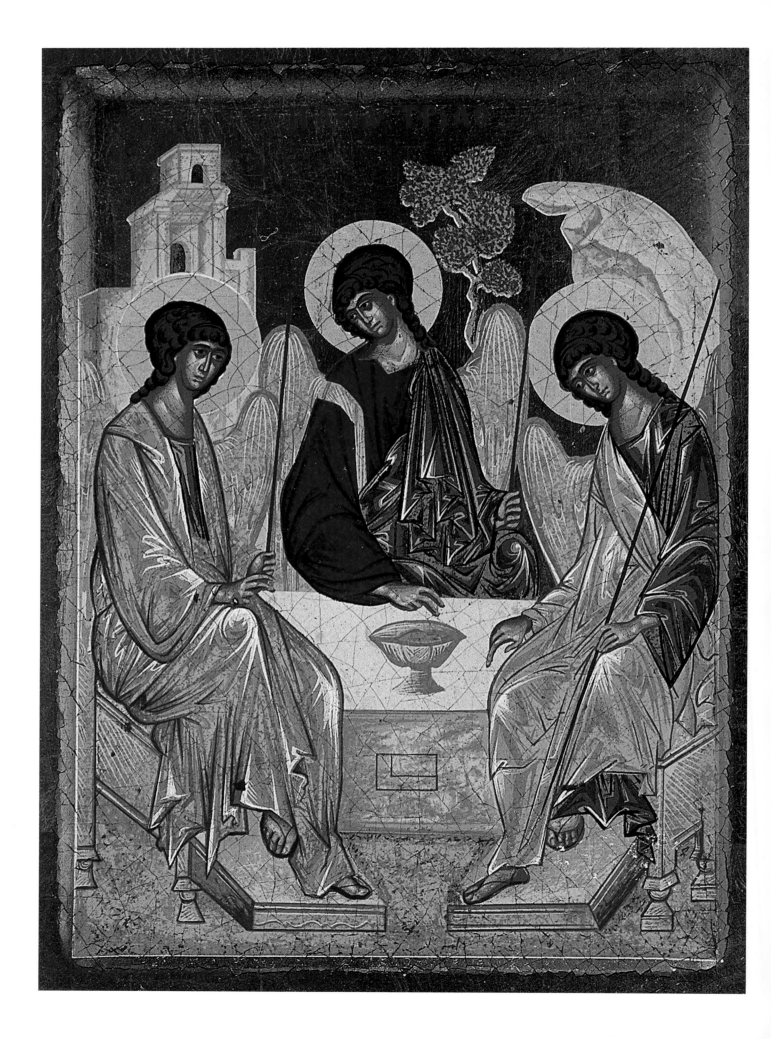

Prayers ∽ THE ICON OF THE TRINITY

GLORY TO YOU, O OUR GOD, GLORY TO YOU.

O Heavenly King, Consoler, Spirit of Truth, everywhere present and filling all things, Treasury of Blessings and Giver of Life: Come dwell within us, cleanse us of every stain, and save our souls, O good one!

Holy God, Holy Mighty, Holy Immortal, have mercy on us (three times).

Glory be to the Father and to the Son and to the Holy Spirit, both now and forever, and to ages of ages. Amen.

O Most Holy Trinity, have mercy on us; Lord, wash away our sins; Master, forgive us our transgressions; Holy One, visit us and heal our infirmities, for your name's sake.

Lord have mercy (three times).

Glory be to the Father and to the Son and to the Holy Spirit, both now and forever and unto the ages of ages. Amen.

Our Father in heaven, hallowed be your name. Your kingdom come; your will be done on earth as it is in heaven. Give us this day our daily bread and forgive us our sins as we forgive those who sin against us. Save us from the time of trial, and deliver us from evil.

For yours is the kingdom and the power and the glory, Father, Son, and Holy Spirit, now and forever, and unto ages of ages. Amen.

The Trinity of Uglic. Rublev, Andrei (1360–c.1430). Mount Athos, 1999. Courtesy of the Brothers of the Christian Schools/De La Salle Institute.

On Prayer

❧

    We should begin by remaining quiet for a few moments till we are no longer preoccupied by our ordinary worries. Then we should attentively say with our hearts open to God this prayer:

Heavenly King, Consoler, Spirit of Truth, you who are present everywhere and fill everything, source of good and giver of life, come dwell within us, cleanse us from every stain, and in your goodness save our souls.

The Holy Spirit lifts our spirit and leads us by the hand when we are weak. He enlightens those who have been purified from their faults. Thus, souls grow in perfection. He makes us spiritual by communion with himself. When a ray of light strikes pure crystal, it illumines it throughout. Our souls too, when they are bearers of the Spirit, become "spiritual" and spread grace to others.

    All good things spring from this single source. Future things can be foreseen, mysteries understood, hidden things uncovered. From this source we receive charismatic gifts and a share in the life of heaven where all join in singing God's praise. Through the Holy Spirit comes the joy of dwelling forever with God, whose nature we share to the point that we have "become God." —Saint Basil, *Treatise on the Holy Spirit*

✑ Life cannot be separated from prayer. Without it, life is devoid of something essential. It becomes uninteresting and shallow. It will have only two dimensions, space and time. Our horizons will not extend beyond our immediate surroundings. We will think of the people around us as ordinary, separated from the awesome and everlasting destinies that are theirs. Prayer is important because it allows us to see that each thing within our purview has something everlasting and enormous in it.

The world we live in is not a secular, unsanctified world. True, we can easily look on it casually, without being aware of the sacredness God has lovingly conferred on it. The life and death of his only Son shows how much the world is worth. Praying opens our eyes. All the things and people we meet are precious for us, because God loves them. Not to pray is to leave God out of his world. We are unaware that it is toward God that all parts of his creation are reaching out. Without this sense we are blind to the world in which we live.

When we get up in the morning, we should place ourselves in the presence of God and say: "Lord, bless me and this day now about to begin." We should think of the unknowable expanse of the new day as a gift from God. This implies something very deep: Nothing that will take place during the day is separate from what God wants. Without any exception, whatever happens will be part of what God wants you to live through in his presence, with his charity, his compassion, his creative understanding, and his courage permeating any situation in which you may find yourself. You are the one God has placed there to do the work of a Christian, to be a part of the body of Christ, to act in his place.

When the evening comes and you once more place yourself before God and review the day, you will be able to sing God's praise, glorify him, thank him, weep for others, and weep for yourself. Once you begin to unite your days with your prayer in this way, they will never be separated and life will become like fuel feeding a fire that will always become warmer and brighter.

You yourself will become the burning bush that scripture speaks about. —Archbishop Anthony Bloom, *Pray Now*

∽ It is possible for us to have the fullness of salvation this very day if we want it firmly, because we are not so tied to the business of this world that we cannot find the occasion to do what is right. On the contrary, it is easy for us to get a hold on salvation through the whole course of the day if we are just willing to sing with our mind alert this verse of David: "In the morning hear my voice, in the morning I will stand before you and you will look on me" (Ps 5), and at nine o'clock say, "Take not your spirit from me" (Ps 51), and at noon, "You will not fear the arrow that flies by day, nor the destruction that wastes at noonday" (Ps 91). At three o'clock we can say, "Incline your ear, O Lord, and answer me" (Ps 86). In the evening we can say, "Bless the Lord, O my soul"—not to mention all that happens before or after.

—Saint Theodore the Studite, *The Great Catechesis*

∽ Our prayers are restless in the beginning. To use the words of Péguy, we should not pray like geese waiting for the mash that fattens them. Men and women are emotional. They tend to pour out their whole psychic energy. Masters of the spiritual life advise us to spend the time of prayer in reading psalms and similar texts lest we become bored. This happens because we think of prayer as a monologue. Those same masters also condemn prolixity. A single word of the publican stirred the Lord to mercy. A single word filled with faith saved the good thief. Chattering away breaks the watchful silence of our mind. The Lord's Prayer is very short, but it contains what alone is necessary. Great saints sometimes restrict themselves to the name of Jesus, but in that name they see his whole kingdom.

—Paul Evdokimov, *La Priere de l'Eglise d'Orient*

⁓ "Pray without ceasing," says Saint Paul, because prayer is the deepest manifestation of our life and the most personal of all our actions. "Enter into your room, close the door, and pray to your Father who is in that secret place." This is an invitation to enter into oneself and make a shrine there. The "secret place" is the human heart. The depth of our spiritual life depends on how personal our prayer is and how it flows in and out of our life. It is also in our prayer that we come to know ourselves.

Jesus "rose long before dawn, went out into a lonely place and prayed." The lonely place (desert) in the thought of the great ascetics comes to mean a quiet state of mind that permits us to concentrate. It is under these circumstances, when we have learned to be quiet, that true prayer takes place. Something mysterious comes to visit us. To hear the language of the Word we must learn to hear his silence and above all dwell in it, for it is the language of the world to come. "Silence of the mind" is superior to meditation. The judgment of the masters is unequivocal on this point. If we do not succeed, if we cannot make a place in our life for silence and concentration, we cannot come to a higher way that allows us to pray in public places. Prayer makes us aware that part of our existence is submerged in what is around us and that we are subject to worry and distraction, while another part of ourselves observes all this with amazement and pity. A worried man makes the angels smile.

—Paul Evdokimov, *La Priere de l'Eglise d'Orient*

⁓ That is how I go about now, ceaselessly repeating the Prayer of Jesus, which is more precious and sweet to me than anything in the world. At times I do as much as forty-three or forty-four miles a day, and I do not feel that I am walking at all. I am aware only of the fact that I am saying my Prayer. When the bitter cold pierces me, I begin to say my Prayer more earnestly and I get warm all over. When hunger begins to over-come me, I call more often on the Name of Jesus, and I forget my wish for food. When I fall ill and get rheumatism in my back and legs, I fix my thoughts on the Prayer and do not notice the pain. If anyone harms me I have only to think, "How sweet is the Prayer of Jesus!" and the injury and the anger alike pass away and I forget it all. I become a sort of half-conscious person. I have no cares and no interests. The fussy business of the world I would not give a glance to. The one thing I wish for is to be alone, and all by myself to pray, to pray without ceasing; and doing this, I am filled with joy. God knows what is happening to me! Of course all this is sensuous or, as my departed staretz said, an artificial state that follows naturally on routine. But because of my unworthiness and stupidity I dare not venture yet to go further, to learn and make my own spiritual prayer within the depths of my heart. I await God's time. And meanwhile I rest my hope on the prayers of my departed staretz. Although I have not yet reached that ceaseless spiritual prayer which is self-acting in the heart, yet I thank God I now understand the meaning of those words I heard in the Epistle—"Pray without ceasing."

I noticed that interior prayer bears fruit in three ways: in the Spirit, in the feelings, and in revelations. In the first, for instance, in the sweet-ness of the love of God, inward peace, gladness of mind, purity of thought, and the sweet remembrance of God. In the second, in the pleas-ant warmth of the heart, fullness of delight in all one's limbs, the joyous bubbling in the heart, lightness and courage, the joy of living, power not to feel sickness and sorrow. And afterward, light given to the mind, understanding of the holy scripture, knowledge of the speech of created things, freedom from fuss and vanity, knowledge of the joy of the inner life, and finally certainty of the nearness of God and of his love for us.

—*The Way of the Pilgrim*

∾ So we went to visit the Greeks and they took us to the place where they worshiped their God. We did not know whether we were in heaven or on earth. For there is nothing on earth like what we saw there, nothing so beautiful. It is indescribable. All we know is that it is there that God dwells among men. Their worship surpasses that of all other countries. No, we cannot forget that beauty; because once anyone knows what sweetness is, bitterness is unbearable. That is why we can no longer stay here.

—"Chronicle of Nestor," *The First Russian Christians*

Worship in the Orthodox Church

✆ The beauty and richness of Orthodox worship make it something distinct from all the rest of Christianity. In it spiritual beauty is joined to a beauty that belongs to this world.

This worship is "heaven on earth"; it shows forth the beauty of the spiritual world. In an Orthodox service beauty has its own distinct place. It should be thought of as the glory of God filling the church. It is parallel to nothing other than prayer and moral example. By its own inherent tendency, Beauty draws us; it has the power of something exemplary and is thereby capable of drawing our minds and hearts. It makes the Church lovable.

During the Christmas service we do not merely commemorate the birth of Christ, but truly Christ is born in a mysterious manner, just as he rises at Easter. The same is true of the Transfiguration, the Entry into Jerusalem, the Sacrament of the Last Supper, the Passion, Burial, and Ascension of Christ, and again of all the events in the life of the Holy Virgin from her Nativity to her Assumption. Worship is synonymous with the life of the Church. In it she makes present for us the Incarnation as it mysteriously unfolds. The Lord continues to live in the Church in the same way he once did on earth and as he continues to do for all time. The Church has power to bring to life these sacred memories. As a result we are made present-day witnesses and sharers in them. It is especially during the reading of the gospel during the liturgy that this transformation becomes possible.

The joy and exaltation of Easter night transports us into the life of the world to come, the joy of joys, the joy without evening.

—S. Bulgakov, *Orthodoxy*

✍ The term "worship" does not have the same meaning when it refers to Christian liturgy as it does when we are talking of pagan or even Jewish worship. It is not some accepted adjustment of the balance between the sacred and the profane, some transaction between God and men that validates the life of men by attaching it to what is sacred. Christian liturgy is an epiphany, a setting out for all to see of something now present, something that is already given, a share of the kingdom brought about by Christ and realized in the coming of the Holy Spirit. No, it is not some form of worship, even a new one, which the Lord once inaugurated. It is the kingdom of God that he opened for men. It is a new life, and not some new religion he gave us. It is the possibility of coming to his table in his kingdom, which he established in this world. The name he gave this opportunity, this life, this ascent, and this communion, is none other than the Church. This means that liturgy by its nature belongs to the world outside of time.

—A. Schmemann, *Historical Aspects of Christian Worship*

Notes on the Icon of Christ

✧

In the Old Testament, before the Incarnation, God summoned his people by the command: "Hearken, O Israel." The basic element of Hebrew religion was the word, to be read, meditated on—day and night, in the heart, according to the Psalmist—proclaimed, and transmitted verbally so it could be heard. God did manifest in the burning bush, in the words of the prophets, but his face remained hidden, inaccessible. It was forbidden to make an image of him because no one has ever seen God. To portray him would be idolatry.

"Hearken, O Israel" is still being said insistently to us, but after the Incarnation something more has been added; it is the "Come and see" which Christ spoke to the first two disciples when they asked him, "Where do you live?" He did not give them his address—did Christ ever have one? He asked them to open their eyes so that they could know him in an entirely different way. Christ continually looks with compassion on the sufferings of men and women, on their weakness, and, in response, he invites them to open their eyes wider, to enlarge their way of seeing things. This applies to the world around us but also to the inner private world of each one of us. (What else is a saint but somebody who sees his or her own heart as it really is?) The importance of our eyes stands out in the many times Christ cured the blind and also in the fact that it was promised to Simeon that he would not die until he had seen Christ. Jesus told Martha, "If you believe you will see the glory of God" (see John 11:40). Most striking is the promise in the final beatitude: "Blessed are the pure of heart because they will see God."

Because of the Incarnation it is now possible for everything about us to be involved in worshiping God; this includes our intelligence, our heart, and the senses that have so great a role to play in our spiritual life. God has already been heard, touched, and seen, since he once walked on earth and lived as a man among his disciples. Hence we can picture him. The Old Testament command not to make a graven image held so long as God had not shown us his face. Before this, any image of him had to be no more than a figment of the human imagination with no connection to reality. The prohibition did not apply to images of angels, because in the case of Jacob a man had seen one. Therefore two cherubim were engraved on the Ark of the Covenant.

Consider carefully this text from the Gospel of John: "Whoever sees me sees him who sent me" (John 12:45). This is the charter that justifies the iconographer's art. It is primarily an act of prayerful adoration. The Master was present for his disciples to look at, to see. They knew his features by heart; every day they were in heartwarming contact with him, and through him with God. What his visible presence did for them, an icon of Christ does for us. What they saw and felt we also experience when our eyes turn toward his face. Through the Son's face, we see the Father. The Holy Spirit appears only in symbols: a dove, or a tongue of fire. The face of God appears for us through the Son. We see his individual face, singular and personal, easily recognizable by us no matter how many representations of him there are scattered over the whole earth.

The beautiful face before us is called the icon "not made by hands." It is the face whose

imprint was left on Veronica's veil. It is left to each of us to discover the riches hidden in it. We cannot fail to see the profound peace that shines forth from Christ's eyes and is evident in the serenity and majesty of his features so reverently set in harmonious balance by the painter. Christ is present for each one of us in this icon. We can see him present to us, even awaiting us in an open and kindly manner. We can expect to find in Christ's gaze a source of grace, a reassurance and an assurance of counsel in troubled moments of our life. By returning the gaze that looks on us we renew our intimacy with God.

Because of the moral weakness, decadence, or spiritual apathy present in people, some icon painters felt it necessary to show Christ in awesome majesty looking at us as a judge. This is how he is seen in the cupola of some Byzantine churches, notably in Daphne.

There have been tragic periods when life was inhuman and cruelty was present everywhere. For example, in the thirteenth century there were the Tartar invasions in Russia. Then Christ was painted in a way that rekindled hope and offered consolation. Our icon is full of the mercy and compassion needed by the faithful.

The twentieth century has experienced great extremes. It seems to be a time of moral laxity and spiritual apathy, but it has also been a time of cruel wars spread over the whole world, of savage concentration camps, of people forced to wander far from their homes, and of famine lasting over many years. Let this image of Christ who himself underwent torture bring us by its loving kindness a reassuring sense of his gentleness and peace.

Prayers ∽ THE ICON OF CHRIST

You, O Christ, are the true light that enlightens and sanctifies everyone who comes into this world! Sign us with the light of your face, that we may recognize in it that light beyond our reach. And by the prayers of your Most Pure Mother and all the saints, direct our steps in the performance of your commandments.

That we may ever give glory to you, your eternal Father, and your all-holy, good, and life-giving Spirit, now and forever, and unto ages and ages.

Face of Christ. The Icon Not Made by Hands. Mount Athos, 1999. Courtesy of the Brothers of the Christian Schools/ De La Salle Institute.

Notes on the Icon of the Mother of God: "Mother Most Tender"

❧

Icons of the Mother of God are probably more widespread and more cherished than any others. One finds them in churches and in homes everywhere. "Love and devotion to the Virgin are the heart and soul of Orthodox piety. They give life and warmth to the whole Church" (Father Serge Bulgakov).

Mary brings her own womanly sensitivity to bear by her interceding for us with the Savior. Realizing that this is so, our feelings toward God also grow warm.

The icon painters show her with her son because her whole meaning and her place in the Church derive from her relationship to him. The scriptures show that she plays a twofold role: she is indispensable because without her free consent the Incarnation could not have taken place, and she is the quiet contemplative who meditates on all that happens and is constantly attentive so that none of it happens without her attention to it. "Mary kept all these things in her heart." The icon allows us to see quite clearly her maternal love and protectiveness. Mary felt all that mothers feel; she

knew joy and she underwent pain, most evidently when she stood on Golgotha.

The love between mother and son seen in this icon is among the most perfect expressions of human love. Christ's face is already that of an adult, and the love he shows toward the one who bore him is both childlike and virile. The presence of both these feelings lends an unmistakable seriousness to the icon. We are being introduced into a higher realm of feeling.

Mary is wearing a mantle of royal purple with golden fringes. One thinks of her queenship extending over all creatures. The three stars (only two of which are visible) signify virginity before, during, and after the birth of her son. Mary's face is grave and stamped with deep refinement—what used to be called nobility—and her head is surrounded by a brownish-gold halo. Her nose is long and thin and her eyes are directed toward a world that lies beyond what the icon can show. She is wholly absorbed in what she sees and there are traces of deep concern. Her head is gently bent toward Jesus, who is sitting upright in her

hands. Love is expressed in the nearness of his cheek to hers. One of his hands holds onto her veil and with the finger of his other hand he gently touches her lips, as if he were trying to still a word of sorrow. He reassures and consoles her. Scripture keeps respectful silence about the feelings between the two, but what writing fails to express is suggested here in the icon. One sees something of the feeling of a son who, just before he died, concerned himself with his mother's future. Speaking to his beloved disciple and his mother from the cross, he said: "Son, behold thy mother, and Mother, behold thy son."

In this love of Jesus for his mother, deeply personal though it is, there also shines through his love, God's love, for all people exemplified in Mary. God's love for all people, his "philanthropy," makes him join the image of God to the human image. Mary was the place where these two were joined.

This icon brings before us the teaching of two ecumenical councils: Ephesus (A.D. 431),

which taught that Mary was truly the Mother of God, and Chalcedon (A.D. 451), which taught that the two natures in Christ, his humanity and his divinity, are united without separation or confusion. The Virgin is there to bear witness to the truth of these dogmas. There before us she is present with her divinized flesh. We also see her son who is at the same time God and son of her human flesh, identical in kind with that of all humanity. This is an icon of human love and of the deepest theological truth.

Mary bears witness to Christ's twofold nature and she intercedes for all men and women. She holds an indispensable place in liturgical prayers and in the litanies and other prayers of the Church. This rich theological teaching is expressed well in one of the hymns sung at Vespers:

> How can we fail to marvel, most venerable Lady, at your motherhood? In it divine and human nature are united.
>
> You knew not man, most pure Virgin, but you bore a Son who had no mortal father, born before all ages of a Father, but without a mother.
>
> Born of you he underwent no change, nor confusion, nor division; instead, he preserves intact what belongs to each of his natures. Do you, O sovereign Virgin and Mother, beg him to save the souls of those who profess the true faith when they recognize you as the Mother of God.

Prayers ∽ THE ICON OF THE MOTHER OF GOD

I place all my trust in you, O Mother of God. Place the veil of your motherly protection over me, your humble and unworthy servant.

O virgin Theotokos, do not disdain me for all my sins, for I need your help and intercession. I put all my trust in you, O Mother of God: have mercy on me.

O all-glorious and ever-virgin Mother of Christ, our God: Take our prayers to your divine Son, that, for your sake, he will save our souls.

*Madonna of Vladimir.
Eleventh–twelfth-century
Russian icon. Tretyakov Gallery,
Moscow, Russia. Courtesy of
Scala/Art Resource, NY.*

Afterword

〜※〜

This book is about faith and prayer. It tells us how the truths of faith are made to shine forth anew each year for all to see as the cycle of the Church's liturgy unfolds.

These pages have brought before our eyes (1) selected texts sung as an act of worship during each of the successive feasts celebrated in the Byzantine liturgy; they are offered on behalf of all the earth to the God who, out of love, made and preserves it; (2) short commentaries on these prayers by masters of the spiritual life as it has been experienced in the Eastern tradition of a once-undivided Church; these commentaries are records of what the liturgy has produced in the lives and minds of those who have allowed themselves to be formed by it; their thoughts are in turn an invitation for us to meditate on what has been granted them to see; and (3) reproductions of the icons proper to each of the great feasts; they are visible witnesses to the faith proclaimed in the texts. There is a reciprocal influence of texts on icons and of icons on the sung texts. Together they renew in our minds and hearts the great events in the history of our salvation.

Though the Byzantine liturgy attained its final form somewhere between the twelfth and fourteenth centuries, it has been enriched constantly by new contributions. It shines forth as a rich structure that astounds us by the perspectives it brings before our minds. The whole fateful drama of humanity's movement through the fall to the fulfillment of God's promise of salvation is played out in the feasts of the church year. The pity felt by God the Father for humanity leads him to send his Son and the Spirit of his love to free those enslaved by sin and to restore them to their original dignity. Those who have participated in the liturgical ceremonies from childhood have thereby been initiated into the knowledge of these mysteries. A learned Russian monk once said, "The words the choir sings are a genuine theological education." Those who follow these words can draw on a storehouse that contains a thousand years of meditation springing from the trials of martyrs, from wars and invasions. Liturgical texts are a faithful mirror that shows the wisdom and beauty of God shining forth amid the vicissitudes of human history.

It is not easy to choose when one is faced with such great richness. The limitations of a short book require that we concentrate on the high points of God's self-revelation and draw on those commentaries that help us see the relevance of revealed doctrines to everyday life. The texts found in this book obviously provide only a brief sketch of Byzantine worship. Nevertheless, by basing itself exclusively on the liturgical presentation of important Christian truths, this book provides the reader with a sense of how the whole of revelation concurs in the fulfillment of God's purposes for humanity. Some readers will find in what they read here sufficient help to guide them on their way. Others will wish to look at other writings in their search for more complete understanding of the mysteries of our religion.

A Book for Those in Search of God

Why do we need this book? There are many others like it already in existence. They too are filled with words and beautiful pictures capable of inspiring us. Furthermore, some may ask what good it does to encourage people to undertake meditative prayer in a world that seems almost exclusively bent on putting up buildings, or producing goods to be bought and sold. Anyone can see that the cities where we live are full of injustice, hunger, and petty wars. What urgency is there for liturgical prayer just now? These grave questions inevitably arise whenever we think of the relation of the Church to the world, but, despite everything, these concerns should not absorb all our attention. A Christian's life is centered on God and we should not forget him. "Lord to whom can we go? You have the words of eternal life" (John 6:68). God's word is an absolute priority for us; it alone is urgent and irreplaceable. Conse-quently, whatever brings us nearer to that word, whatever illumines it, or helps us to interpret it correctly, or enables us to nourish ourselves by it is important. In the words of Saint Paul, "All things have been created in him and for him" (Col 1:16). This is the real perspective from which we can help to build the "city of man."

Modern people are slaves to time. They want to do everything, but they have time for nothing, especially not for prayer. They are always in a hurry, as if the thought of death were haunting them, but the faster they go the more they need to flee. We are offering such people a book of prayers to be read slowly and attentively. What we propose is a change of rhythm in the breathless rush of daily life, or at least a pause when we can allow ourselves some moments free from the tyranny of what from every direction so peremptorily demands our immediate attention. The pause we are speaking about must last long enough for us to refocus our thoughts. It need not last long. The centurion asked the Lord for only one word to effect the cure of his servant (Matt 8:8). We too must constantly seek such a word, but calmly, without being frenzied or in a hurry. The word we need may leap out suddenly as we turn a page, but it will find its way to our heart and shed light on some event of our life. A hurried, inattentive reading of these pages would be useless; they need to be savored slowly, ruminated on in peace.

If we leave an empty space in the all-too-full course of our daily life and prepare ourselves to read some passage thoughtfully, a presence will come to fill that void and we will know the joy of that presence.

The Bible implies that knowing someone's name makes the person named present to us. The Jews were filled with fear and trembling before the Eternal, and so they never pronounced the divine name. But in the New Testament we call on God constantly as Father, and as Christ Jesus ("so that at the name of Jesus every knee should bend in heaven and on earth and under the earth"—Phil 2:10), and as the Holy Spirit ("who is given to those who ask"—Luke 11:13).

In the Eastern Church every single prayer, whether individual or collective, begins with an invocation of the Holy Spirit who gives us the power to pronounce the name of the Lord (1 Cor 12:3). A meditative reading of the liturgical texts puts us in the presence of the Savior at work within our sinful world. God is then present for us and we are part of the communion of the Church, that is, of all those men and women who have filled their minds with these texts, all those who have been caught up as they prayed over them, all those who have fulfilled their destiny through these prayers.

An important aspect of our life ought to be taking the time to see how beautiful the world is. We need to feel the wonder of those landscapes where trees, grass, birds, and the sun sing the glory of the world. We must also learn about suffering when we are by a sick person's bedside, or talking with a neighbor in trouble. We then must find friendly words warmed by life as it exists all around us. We should live as much as possible in the presence of God, even through the loneliness of the night ("I slept, but my heart was awake"—Song of Songs 5:2). Saint John Chrysostom tells his disciples "to dwell in the name of Jesus, so that the heart can absorb Jesus and Jesus can absorb our heart, so that two become one." This book will have fulfilled its purpose if it can serve as a guide in our search for what alone is necessary.

To live in God involves humility, openness to the divine will, and a desire to be enlivened, with a heart stretched out toward fulfillment.

Once a woman complained to a Russian bishop that she could no longer find words to express her prayer and she felt helpless in a spiritual desert. The bishop told her to sit down with her knitting before her icons and to say nothing. Little by little, peace came over her and words began to be formed on her lips. This woman had allowed herself to be enlivened by the power that shone forth from her icons. The great contemplatives allowed themselves to be overshadowed in this way by God's presence, and they accompanied their prayer by prolonged ascetical practices. In that way it became possible for them to say: "It is no longer I who live, but it is Christ who lives in me" (Gal 2:20).

Preliminary Remarks on the Liturgy: Heaven on Earth

This expression—"heaven on earth"—was used to describe the liturgy by Father Serge Bulgakov, a great Russian theologian of the beginning of the last century. The surest way of coming to know Orthodoxy in depth is to come to know the richness of its service: "Come and see." The liturgy is a source of life and joy. From the moment that Christ came down to dwell among us we have been invited to join in celebrating the life he continues to live among us. When we strive to do so, we have in the liturgy a foretaste of the heavenly banquet and a pledge of everlasting glory. The familiarity of our relationship with God, disturbed by Adam's fall, is once again reestablished. We can turn to God and dare to say with confidence, "Our Father."

By the same token, each of us reestablishes our own oneness with the community around us, between ourselves as members and the body to which we belong, between ourselves as individual Christians and all humanity: "Love your neighbor as yourself." It is an error to want to separate the love of Christ from loving all men and women; it is wrong to divide the Church and the world. Saint John Chrysostom tells us that the mystery on the altar cannot be dissociated from the mystery of our brother. This remains true no matter how many times the Church has been tempted to put all its emphasis on the first to the detriment of the second great commandment. The now-familiar prayer that Christ left for us tells us that we will be pardoned for our offenses to the degree that we pardon those who have offended us. "Before you offer your gift on the altar, go first and be reconciled with your brother or sister" (see Matt 5:23–24). Love of God passes through love for our neighbor. No one can say he loves God if he hates the brother or sister he meets in everyday life, that is to say, anyone who is poor, or ill, or in the extreme situations experienced by people under torture for the sake of justice, or who are otherwise deprived of happiness and love.

The Christian Church had its beginning in an upper room when Christ, surrounded by his twelve apostles, celebrated the Jewish Passover in a manner that transformed it ever after into something utterly new. (In Orthodox churches this "upper" room is brought to mind by the elevation of the platform where the inconostasis and the altar of the church are situated.) This meal links heaven and earth. It is the focus around which two essential elements are always present: the hearing of the word and the distribution of the bread and wine which is at once a material action and the living sign of our inner communion with God.

Liturgy and the Bible

The word "liturgy" means an action performed by the members of a group. We can rightly extend this meaning to signify a biblical drama, since the liturgy we celebrate is a communal service during which we make present events spoken of in the scriptures by reading, singing, and gestures. What we do manifests the whole divine plan for our salvation. In our liturgical celebration we dramatically reenact the content of the scriptures as interpreted by the ecumenical councils, by the lives of the saints, by the Church Fathers, and by the tradition of the Church alive over the centuries. The origin of our worship is the scripture. We celebrate its message in ever-new forms whose meaning is never exhausted. Liturgy, then, is an all-inclusive action where men and women of today enter as fully into the work of salvation as did those who lived two thousand years ago.

Can Modern Men and Women Relate to the Liturgy?

Our liturgy had its beginnings in an agricultural society. Therefore, it is full of references to the cosmic meaning of wheat, wine, oil (for anointing), water, flowers (at Pentecost), and fruit (for the Transfiguration). All these natural things have meaning as signs of how holiness can come into our life. They remind us that our first parents carried the rest of creation with them in their fall from grace. That is why nature "has been groaning in labor pains" (Rom 8:22) "in hope that . . . [it] will be set free from its bondage to decay" (Rom 8:21).

These once powerful cosmic symbols have little meaning for us or for our contemporaries. We live in an industrialized world far from such thoughts, but it is easy to rediscover the sacred in other parts of our experience. One has only to think of loneliness, friendship, the meaning and/or the meaninglessness of life, injustice, famine, various forms of suffering, imprisonment, moments of happiness. We have moved from the cosmic symbolism that remains central to the way sacraments signify to realms of experience inseparable from modern life that have a no less profound spiritual meaning for us.

The liturgy sheds light on that inner world, just as it did on the natural perspectives of our ancestors. It brings our everyday world also to the foot of Christ's Cross in the full understanding that he took on himself the tragedy of human suffering, including death and final victory. "By death Christ has overcome death."

In its liturgy the Church extends its compassion to the whole universe, including all humanity. Masters of the spiritual life are unanimous in saying, "You will be saved if you save your neighbor." Though the Church is not of this world, it exists for the world. The sacrifice it offers in the liturgy is "for all men and for all women" (the words said during the liturgy after the consecration to signify those for whom the eucharistic sacrifice is being offered). In saying these words, the Church is acting in conformity with the plan of God "who did not send his Son to judge the world, but that the world might be saved."

Consequently, every liturgy can be lived out "in the joy and exaltation that carry us into the world to come, into the joy that surpasses all joys, the joy that has no evening" (Serge Bulgakov).

Thoughts on the Power of Beauty: The Lord Is Clothed in Splendor

Our God is a God who allows us to see glimpses of him, who gives us intimations of what he is like. As a psalm verse sung at Vespers says, "The Lord reigns; he is clothed in splendor."

Not only does beauty belong to the nature of God as the source of all created beauty in the world, but it belongs to his actions, especially to his sacrificial love. A verse in the Anaphora (canon) of the liturgy expresses this fact: "You are perfect in holiness and magnificent is your glory, you who have so loved the world that you gave your only Son so that whoever believes in him should not perish, but have eternal life." This beauty can be communicated to men and women and they can quench their thirst by sharing in it.

The final prayer of thanksgiving at the end of the liturgy asks God "to sanctify those who love the beauty of your house." We need the power of our intelligence to understand the word of God and the power of charity as the essential means of leading an upright life and to spur us to concern for our neighbor's needs, but we also need something else that is often overlooked, the power to open ourselves to our God, whose endless goodness is replete with wonder. He has brought us from nothingness to existence. We can best respond to this enormous kindness by offering thanks, that is to say, the Eucharist. ("Eucharist" in Greek means "thanks.") The feeling of at-one-ness leaps out from page after page of the Bible, starting in Genesis when God "saw [that what he had made] was good," and continuing through the Psalmist's awe before the infinite mercy of God (Ps 118). The New Testament shows us the adoration of the Magi and lets us see the won-

94

der of those pagans who, having received the Spirit, extolled God (Acts 10:46). Wonder and amazement are not forms of action, but they are a way of being through which men and women can find their own true center and allow themselves to be transformed while they witness the pure spontaneity of God giving himself to us. Such an experience is the exact opposite of our all-too-frequent attempts to "do something."

These magnificent sentiments are not the only truths about the world. We should not forget the ugliness that often disfigures the world. Its most distinctive form is that Satanic destructiveness embodied in a calculated refusal to serve God or neighbor. Satan is the light-bearer who was plunged into darkness. From him spring those manifestations of hate which from time to time plague our world and plunge it into continuous misery. One of these plagues is widespread famine, and not only for bread, but also for the nourishment that feeds the heart and gives the spirit a sense of purpose in life. Another manifestation is arrogance and torture and the doctrinaire fanaticism responsible for concentration camps and penitentiaries that are the dwelling places of nothing but despair. Also there are cruel asylums for the insane. In the gloomy atmosphere of these hells, men and women exist without hope. There is also in many minds an absence of anything they can admire, and so they pass their days and nights in an atmosphere that mocks them and leaves only a feeling of sullen resentment and a nihilism indistinguishable from despair.

Dostoevsky knew the darker side of our spirit. Nevertheless, he dared utter one striking prophecy: "Beauty will save the world." What beauty can do this? Not the fleeting beauty of things that perish, or esthetic satisfaction. Our response to beautiful form in works of art is at best ambiguous. The beauty that can change us is the one whose roots lie in something beyond us, something far away. Beauty wounds us because it is fleeting and stirs up in us a nostalgia for a paradise we have lost. That is why we are so deeply moved by it. Dostoevsky thinks beauty is fragile and that it never constrains us. We are freely drawn to it. Ugliness, though, imposes itself on us without hesitation or shame. Beauty is precarious; we must win our way to it by struggle. Even though it exists in some protected spots here and there, we still must search for traces of it in our neighbor, in society. It is ever to be found as it springs from the hand of a generous Creator.

Icons: Places Where God's Beauty Dwells

In the Bible God sometimes appears as fire and sometimes as light. We have both the burning bush and the cloud that preceded the Jewish people on their journey from Egypt. We see this brilliant cloud with its transfiguring light again on Mount Tabor. All these are manifestations of God's glory.

God also makes himself known to us as a Person who shows us his face: "He who has seen me has seen the Father" (John 14:9). According to scripture, human beings were created in God's image. By the Incarnation God revealed to us the face of God, but by the same token he has shown us the face of a human being who is like God. This is the justification for painting icons which would have been unthinkable and even forbidden in the Old Testament when God had not yet removed the veil that concealed his face. It was possible to have angels sculpted on the Ark of the Covenant because they were somehow accessible, as we see in the episode of Jacob wrestling with an angel.

Christ's humanity is, properly speaking, the image of the Godhead. This is what the Fathers of the Seventh Ecumenical Council (A.D. 787) saw and proclaimed. Icons make no pretense of being portraits. Details of physiognomy or landscape are not normally intended to be historically accurate. An icon painter tries to make the faces of Christ, the Mother of God, the saints, and the prophets shine forth as perfectly as possible, but as images of God. In Christ's face the likeness is complete. In the faces of other holy people there is a fire that illumines them from within.

We are warned by the Fathers of the Council not to worship icons. We should not treat them as if they were idols. In itself no icon is sacred, but, like holy scripture, it is a path that leads to what it represents. Icons are vehicles of grace that lead to salvation. Icons are the Bible in pictures, just as the stained glass windows in Western cathedrals are said to be. Hence, icons can teach us. They can revive our memory of God wherever we happen to be, at home or in a church, and they can move us to become godlike.

Icons bring us into the presence of what they represent. Esthetic concern for the techniques used in creating them do not obtrude themselves on our attention nor do we concentrate on the "beautiful" in some detached manner. These considerations belong to the perishable world, whereas icons make us aware of the eternal. Plato says beauty is the splendor of truth. This implies that beauty springs forth from the underlying idea that permits it to be.

In the icon of the Nativity we are led beyond the merely factual—the ox and the ass, the shepherds—to the truth that God himself has burst the heavens asunder so that he can be born humbly as a human being. This truth reaches the eyes of our mind. Our fleshly eyes start with the visible and we go beyond it to what God has revealed as his plan for the world. In the center of the icon we see a child born in a dark cave (a symbol of death and all that is hellish in human life) and bringing hope to the darkness of human despair. This is a truth that attains what is eternal and takes us beyond the world of space and time that limits us as we live our earthly lives.

The icon painter ignores the classic laws of artistic proportion. Elongated bodies seem weightless; the line of the underlying landscape is deliberately broken up into geometric forms that no mainline painter before the Cubists of the twentieth century would have found desirable. In icons, temporally distinct incidents are presented simultaneously. We see the birth and the washing of the newborn child, and at the same time we see the arrival of the Magi, the announcement to the shepherds, the temptation of Joseph, and Mary's sad look as she foresees the future. This rearrangement of space and time shows that we are in the presence of a spiritual landscape, inward looking and harmonious, a landscape that invites men and women of every age to contemplate truths that never change. We see theology before us alive with form and color.

Church Fathers frequently say that an icon brings us into the presence of the one represented. Greatness becomes present to us when an icon helps us lift our mind to God. Mighty too is the one who can discover the image of God in the faces of those we see, even when they are great sinners. Saint Seraphim of Sarov had this power. He was a beloved nineteenth-century Russian saint, a witness to the power of Easter joy. He it was who, when he came out to meet a visitor, would look at the person and shout out: "What joy I see before me: Christ is risen!"

God in his measureless mercy sent his only Son into the depths of that hell which threatened to engulf humanity. His Son "humbled himself, and became obedient to the point of death—even death on a cross" (Phil 2:8). The eyes of any truly compassionate human being reflect in a marvelous manner the beauty of God's compassion for his world. This feeling is registered in the faces of holy men and women living here on earth or present in icons. Like a hidden fire it warms our hearts with a sense of God's mighty promises and the love they make possible for us living here below. A contemplative who lived in our time said this well: Given one and only one condition, the world we see would be filled with endless light shining from the faces of those we have loved; they would all have the face of Christ and the face of Christ would resemble theirs; this is the experience that in all humility would be ours in our day-to-day life. And what is the condition that would make all this possible? It is that we find ourselves without restraint in love with the beauty from which all else comes, God himself.

The title of this book is "Light from the East." Those words require an explanation. Everyone knows that light for the world rises in the east, and that for those who live in Western Europe and America the eastern part of the Mediterranean is the birthplace of the three great monotheistic religions: Judaism, Christianity, and Islam. It is from this spot that the message of God's plan for the world began to spread. The founder of Christianity walked on the hills of Palestine and along the shores of its lakes. There he talked to the people he met, and there he cured their infirmities. What we may call an oriental character strongly marks this intimacy with what comes from God, this familiarity with the spiritual in our lives.

However, we must give a much wider geographical extension to this way of looking at things. The light of the liturgy shines on all those who, from Russia to the Middle East and on the African continent, feel a kinship with one another based on their manner of worshiping God. The term "oriental" becomes completely relative. This is true for two reasons. The first is, of course, related to geography. What we call "east" depends on where we are on the planet. (Christianity is a Western religion for the Indian.) The second reason is rooted in history. We need to be warned that "light from the East" does not belong exclusively to the East, because light by its nature diffuses itself as far as possible in all directions.

For the first thousand years of its history, the undivided Church, the unique Church of Christ, shared the light that rose in the east and shone out in the prayers of the liturgy and in other manifestations of our shared faith. Very early on, the West found its own distinctive way. There was a richness of rite and a powerful set of Romanesque images that belonged to the West and manifested a state of mind, a particular language, and a distinct culture. And yet, although forms gradually evolve, the basic source remains the same. In every land, all seek light from above to enlighten the darkness of this world.

May this book serve to bridge the chasm of ignorance that separates us and allow us to see our common roots or—to change the metaphor—build a bridge that will bring us nearer to one another. We are united in adoring the same Savior. We are alike in our overpowering sense that God loves us. Since he sent his Son not to judge but to save a sinful world, we share hope for what is promised us in the gospels. May this book, along with other books that shine out today, be capable of warming the hearts of those who wish to follow the Lord who came to kindle fire on the earth (Luke 12:49).